# THE ART OF BEING A JEW

# The Art
## of Being a Jew

### RABBI MORRIS N. KERTZER

CLEVELAND AND NEW YORK

THE WORLD PUBLISHING COMPANY

Published by *The World Publishing Company*
2231 West 110th Street, Cleveland 2, Ohio

Published simultaneously in Canada by
Nelson, Foster & Scott Ltd.

Library of Congress Catalog Card Number: 62-15714

FIRST EDITION

WP962

To my beloved parents of blessed memory,
David and Pearl Kertzer, who taught me the art . . .

# ACKNOWLEDGMENTS

I AM HAPPY TO RECORD my indebtedness to a number of people whose generous aid, in so many ways, made this book possible.

Mrs. Edyth Miller prepared the entire manuscript with infinite patience and diligence. Among those who generously gave of their time for technical assistance and counsel were Mrs. Maurice Mermey, Mrs. Sheldon Turk, Miss Mary de Haas, Miss Barbara Furth, and Mrs. Michael Harris.

To Mr. Bernard Postal, editor of the *Jewish Digest*, I must express my gratefulness for use of material which has appeared in my monthly column of the *Digest*.

To Sonya Kaufer, for her inestimable editorial aid, I want to record my heartfelt gratitude.

For the encouragement and assistance of my wife, Julia, and for the friendly criticism of my children, Ruth, David, and Jonathan—my loving appreciation.

MORRIS N. KERTZER

*Larchmont, New York*
*May, 1962*

# Contents

## I STILL BELIEVE IN MAN

## REMAKING OUR WORLD

# By Way of an Introduction

DURING MY SEMINARY DAYS, students were required to take turns presenting a trial sermon at our Wednesday class; if it passed muster, they were permitted to preach on the same theme on the following Saturday morning before the seminary congregation.

One Saturday, our homiletics professor, Dr. Mordecai Kaplan, decided to attend our Sabbath services instead of preaching in his own pulpit. After worship, he sharply criticized the student rabbi's presentation.

"But, Dr. Kaplan," the young man protested, "you yourself approved my sermon last Wednesday."

"Ah, yes," replied Dr. Kaplan. "But that was last Wednesday. I'm older now."

In a sense, these observations also represent certain "second thoughts." An earlier book, *What Is a Jew?*, concerned itself primarily with the traditional customs and rituals of Judaism and the meanings behind them. These further reflections are intended to take off from there. For if being a Jew is to represent more than an accident of birth, it must be infused with an ongoing meaning and purpose, and cultivated and refined into a way of life. It is this capacity to distill the wisdom of a glorious past and make it applicable to the demanding present that I view as the greatest challenge—and art—of the modern Jew.

In the chapters that follow, I have tried to set down some thoughts encompassing my essential philosophy about Jews and Judaism. To the reader who asks if this is a valid and

authentic presentation of what Jews believe, I can only respond that I feel it to be an accurate description of the Jewish
spirit.

What I have tried to put into these pages is a taste of modern Judaism. The question for some people will be: Is it
modern or is it Judaism? I believe with all my heart that what
we call modern Judaism is a way of thought and life that
would have appealed to the historic architects of our faith.
Were the prophet Isaiah alive today, or those creative rabbis
of the Talmud, Hillel and Akiba, or the twelfth century's
Moses Maimonides, their views, I think, would be closer to
modern Jewish thought than to classic traditionalism. I often
imagine Maimonides reading such works as Mordecai M.
Kaplan's *Judaism Without Supernaturalism* and saying to himself, "I could have written that!"

Judaism, I maintain, has never been a rigid, unbending
faith. Neither has it been a catchall for every doctrine from
humanist to fundamentalist. It was Professor Solomon Schech-
ter who warned, in the early years of our century, against a
"Judaism of the sane and plausible kind that made no demands on faith" and was so elastic as to be "compatible with
any system of philosophy ever advanced."

In sifting through the many rich veins of Jewish thought
and writing, I have never judged an idea solely by its compatibility with modern thinking. But neither have I been prepared to accept a concept as valid solely because it could be
supported by a Biblical verse, or a sentence in a legal code.
Instead, I have asked myself: What is Judaism really trying
to say to us? What is the major thrust of its spirit as it ad-
dresses itself to man?

One of the luminaries of the nineteenth century, Rabbi
Samson Raphael Hirsch, once described a group of children
he had seen dashing out of their religious school. "Hurrah!"
they shouted. "No religion today! The teacher's sick!" Rabbi
Hirsch was amused by this immature image of religion as a
bitter pill to be swallowed regularly because "it's good for
you." Yet this is often the view of the unsophisticated, to whom

religion is a kind of insistent, demanding force *outside them-selves,* capricious, arbitrary, exacting, authoritarian—a voice which thunders: "This shalt thou do." In this light, religion becomes merely an exercise which one can relegate to a spe-cific time and a specific place, or dodge altogether from time to time. This is not my idea of any religion—and least of all, of Judaism. In *What Is a Jew?* I dwelled at length on the fact that Judaism is neither a body of doctrine nor a theological discipline, but a way of life—and even more accurately, a way of looking at life. Is it a demanding faith? Certainly. But the imperative lies neither in the threat of sacerdotal reprisal nor in a deity equipped with lethal thunderbolts for the un-regenerate.

How easy we find it to attribute our inner promptings to forces within ourselves. Are the moral exactions of my parents inside me, or outside my being? Can I really differentiate be-tween the ethical demands they made upon me during their lifetime and those they continue to make of me—except that the latter are more insistent and more persuasive?

I have long wondered why we distinguish between the immanent conception of God—"God is within us"—and the transcendental conception—"God is outside ourselves." This distinction implies that the former is a subjective, incomplete type of religion. Yet nothing is entirely inside of us; even our physical being is the product of drives external to ourselves. "The God within us," then, must be our consciousness of all that has come to us from the world without.

When spring beckons and every tendon of our being draws us to the eye-lighting treasures of tulips and daffodils, where lies the tyrant that drives us to finish the sonata exercises, to tarry over our books for a few more hours? Toscanini, they say, would cry out to his musicians during rehearsal: "*I* don't ask it; *Beethoven* asks it!"

Who asks it, indeed? That divine magnet, which Jewish tradition poetically calls "the daughter of a voice"—is it "out there" or "in here"? Philosopher Immanuel Kant described it in the ossifying phrase "categorical imperative." Judaism prefers the timeless, spaceless language: "Thus saith the Lord."

The insistent clamor comes from within ourselves, not because we are the *creators* of faith, but because we are its *discoverers*. The art of being a Jew, it seems to me, is the ability to perceive in this universe an inherent force that makes for righteousness, an acute awareness that within the very fabric of our being is a moral force which breathes truth and goodness and beauty into man's experience. Once that discovery is made—and the uniqueness in Judaism is nothing more than the historic fact that Jews have continued the quest ever since Abraham heard the beckoning call, "Look now toward heaven," more than three millenniums ago—we become, in a sense, permanent slaves of goodness and decency. The impulse to build a Kingdom of God comes neither from the lash of a divine taskmaster nor from the promise of a paradise to come. Such sanctions, though timelessly invoked, have yet to make man good. True salvation lies only in the spiritual and intellectual enlightenment of spirit that derives from being at peace with ourselves.

Some might argue that this modern interpretation of Judaism leaves out God. Quite the contrary. To me such a vision of the universe restores God to His loftiest essence. He is no longer a policeman with a stick or a doorkeeper at the gates, but a judge in the purest sense of the word—probing the recesses of our hearts so that we dare not be pretentious, and so ordering His universe that good men everywhere want to play according to His rules.

A considerable portion of this book is based on lectures and sermons given to the members of Larchmont Temple. To these good friends I am grateful not only for their indulgent listening but for their added kindness in affording me the time to share whatever insights I have been able to offer them with this wider audience.

Our prayer book beckons us to "see and welcome all truth, whether shining from the annals of ancient revelations or reaching us through the seers of our own time." It is in this spirit that I have tried to heed the words of a very wise man, Dr. Albert Schweitzer:

"Impart as much as you can of your spiritual being to those who are on the road with you, and accept as something precious what comes back to you from them."

# *The Modern Jew*

# Rabbi and Congregant

HAVING BEEN both rabbi and congregant for many years, I think I can look with the same objectivity through both ends of the binoculars. Whenever I stand in the pulpit I try to keep in mind the silent listeners who, within the imprisonment of their pew, must take chastisement without complaint. (In Washington not long ago, a Catholic Bishop delivered a sermon calling for Federal aid to parochial schools. Three Supreme Court judges sat in the congregation, listening without any hope of refutation.)

A friend of mine, an attorney, was invited to speak in the Midwest, and gave what he regarded as a brilliant address. The Chairman then called on the city's leading rabbi for the benediction. The rabbi rose and said, "Ladies and gentlemen, before offering my prayer, I want to take exception to some of the remarks of the speaker." He then held forth with a number of excoriating comments. Just as my friend rose to offer a rebuttal, the rabbi lowered his voice: "Ladies and gentlemen, the benediction."

I am well aware that this little episode reflects accurately the frustration which all too often envelops the congregant.

Is the rabbi sitting in judgment upon me? Does his rabbinical robe empower him to stand before the altar and catalog *my* sins and *my* transgressions? Has he a private pipeline to God, that he can bespeak with such authority the divine will on such issues as collective bargaining, atomic testing, civil liberties?

Jews know that our faith does not cloak their rabbi with holy immunities. How then is he to avoid the resentment of

his congregants and still perform the tasks he must? To my
way of thinking, perhaps the most indispensable ingredient in
a rabbi's soul is a genuine sense of humility about his calling.

There is only one difficulty with humility: it is a quality we
no longer possess, the moment we are conscious of having it.
The medieval philosopher, Judah Ibn Tibbon, in his great
classic, *Duties of the Heart*, warns us that of all the virtues,
humility is the most elusive. For who is so arrogant as the
human being who, in the secrecy of his own heart, is suddenly overwhelmed with the irrepressible thought: Am I not
wonderfully humble?

For myself, I have a simple measure of a man's essential
humility. Can he laugh at himself? If he can, he sees himself
in the delectable perspective of a frail human being, with a
respectable stock of shortcomings. I like the practice described
by Nehru of India in his autobiography, *Toward Freedom*.
At the beginning of each day, the Prime Minister stands on
his head in front of a mirror. One glimpse of that ridiculous
sight at the outset of a day's work is enough to assure a properly proportioned image of oneself.

Yogi sources are hardly unique in their appreciation of
humility. The Bible describes the greatest figure in human
history in these words: "The man, Moses, was a humble man,
more so than any on the face of the earth." Perhaps the most
important word in that verse is not "humble," but "man."
Moses confronted God "face to face." He braved the loneliness
of Sinai's heights. He defied the mightiest ruler on earth. He
transformed rock into life-giving water. Nevertheless, he was
a *man*. Man can achieve infinite wonders. He can even set
his own man-made stars into the heavens. But he remains—
all of us remain—no more than human. And so the rabbi, in
consonance with the spirit of our faith, can never say, "*You*
have sinned; *you* have acted iniquitously," but always, "*We*
have transgressed; *we* have been guilty."

What then is the relationship between rabbi and congregant? First, I think, the congregant has a right to expect of
his rabbi unswerving guidelines of ethical and moral inspira-

tion. By what standards shall I behave toward my husband or wife, my children, my parents, my fellow students, my employers, my employees? The rabbi, drawing from the infinite well of Jewish wisdom and insight, must provide not only the knowledge of what is right and wrong, for these most often we know ourselves, but, more significantly, the strength of purpose which enables us to follow through. "Why shouldn't I cheat in examinations?" "Why can't I cut corners in the jungle of economic competition?" "Why shouldn't I consider myself and my family before my clients or patients?" These are all very real and pressing questions in our time and society. The rabbi must help to provide meaningful answers.

Every rabbi has had congregants apologize to him for the use of profane or vulgar language in his presence. I think it is because the rabbi is a kind of symbolic conscience. He represents parent, grandparent, the whole sweep of Jewish spiritual tradition. Thus when we do something of which we are somewhat ashamed, a nod in his direction is indicated. (If I thought it would accomplish anything, I would suggest to my fellow rabbis that they present two pictures of themselves to every family in their congregation—one for the office and one for the dining room. Then, when someone is tempted to act deviously in business or to engage in some ungenerous gossip at the dinner table, there might at least be an embarrassed nod in the rabbi's direction.) At any rate, the role of the rabbi as conscience is unquestioned.

How many of us also think of the rabbi as a scholar? Dr. Bernard Bamberger, a leader in the Central Conference of American Rabbis, describes the modern rabbinate as a "new profession." The rabbi of today, Dr. Bamberger points out, has no image of himself as the counterpart of the rabbi of old. Nor do his congregants.

The great Rabbi of Vilna, Elijah, spent eighteen hours a day bent over his books. He begrudged the time wasted in walking to and from the synagogue for prayer. Was not God worshiped by devotions of the mind as well as worship of the heart?

The world of Jewish learning was likened to a vast ocean. Who could encompass it in one lifetime of study? And, unless that sea were constantly traversed—*all* of the sea—it would soon become an uncharted Antarctica. No one, therefore, dared trespass on the sacred hours the scholar-rabbi set aside for mastering the inspired literature of our faith. And it was not study in order to teach. It was study simply because it was important that someone in the world possess such knowledge. Just as we insist that our encyclopedias contain limitless stores of knowledge, regardless of how infrequently some references are consulted, so the Jewish community took immense pleasure in the fact that in its midst someone, unworried, undistracted, and undisturbed, was exploring the wonderful world of Jewish thought.

Still another expectation of the ideal rabbi is that he be a pastor. I know of no greater satisfaction in life than the rewarding knowledge that my words and actions—a silent gesture to a bride and groom, a murmur of condolence to a widow bereaved, a strong arm for the youngster who has lost his way in the blinding world of adolescence—can often bring comfort, aid, and purpose to the people whose lives and hearts I touch.

An old friend of mine, Dr. Arthur Steindler, was regarded as the Einstein of orthopedic surgery. In his more than fifty years of medicine he operated on over thirty thousand patients, many of them hopelessly crippled children. The child's pain was his pain. He said he cried after every operation, and when you looked at his beautifully expressive face you believed him. You asked yourself, How much pain, even vicarious anguish, can one human being endure? To me, Dr. Steindler is the model for every pastor, of every faith.

When we speak of a supporting arm, we mean something more than the encouragement of cleverly turned phrases. The congregant must feel, within the essence of his being, his rabbi's immeasurable reservoir of faith—faith in a just and compassionate God, ever searching, ever wondering, ever grasping for light and truth. For the Jew, who looks to his rabbi not for miracles but for compassion, there is much comfort in this knowledge.

Finally, we come to that aspect of the rabbi's mission to which he owes his name. Above all else, the Jewish minister is a teacher—and a teacher of teachers. Jewish tradition breathes the word "teacher" with almost speechless awe. "He who teaches another human being," says the Talmud, "is as though he were the parent who brought him into the world."

What a striking metaphor that is. The true teacher is the spiritual parent. The parent gives life to the child, the teacher gives meaning to that life. The parent brings the child into the world, the teacher endows that world with purpose, beauty, direction.

Study the history of the synagogue in Jewish life. You will be amazed at the number of times our forefathers thought of their house of God as a place of communion with the divine through study. It was called a *Beth Midrash,* a school, as often as it was called a *Beth Knesset,* a sanctuary.

As a rabbi, I would hope that my congregant would ask me why the poetry of Bialik and Judah Halevi excite me, why the insights of Maimonides and Ahad Ha'am open new vistas of intellectual exploration, why the Bible in Hebrew is so much more moving than the Bible in English (there is a Jewish epigram that speaks of reading a translation as akin to kissing a bride through her veil). I would like my congregant to discover through me what guidance Isaiah and Amos, Akiba and the Baal Shem Tov have for us in meeting the burning social issues of our time.

Of course one is justified in asking me, at this time, "Are you describing one rabbi or five?" I suppose the only answer is to close with the legend about the birth of a great Hasidic master, Rabbi Levi Isaac of Berditchev. There are countless stories of this rabbi's tolerance, his wisdom, his love of people. When someone complained to Rabbi Levi Isaac that his congregants habitually engaged in trifling conversation during worship, he lifted his eyes heavenward and whispered, "Oh! Heavenly Father, what a wonderful people are Thy children.

Even while they're busy talking, they take time out to pray to Thee."

Legend tells us that before Rabbi Levi Isaac came into this world, an emergency meeting was called in Heaven. Satan demanded of the heavenly throne: "Almighty God, is it fair to bring such a perfect saint down to earth? He'll put me, the devil, out of business!" The Almighty reassured Satan: "Please don't worry. I will make this pure soul a rabbi in Israel. He will be so absorbed in communal affairs, you'll have plenty left to do."

# Earthbound or Heavenbound

Some months ago, I invited the members of my confirmation class to express their views on God, religion, and the Jewish faith. The group took me very seriously and penned some challenging and sobering ideas.

These fifteen- and sixteen-year-olds find themselves in earnest disagreement with some of the basic teachings of their parents and their Sunday school, but there is a wholesome quality of humility, even in their rejection.

For example, the most articulate student in the class declared: "I cannot accept most of the Bible as truth. Unless someone can prove it to me, or I can prove it to myself, I cannot believe in a God as the Bible pictures him—a God sitting up there in Heaven. On a Sunday morning or a Sabbath eve, He would have an awfully tough time listening to hundreds of millions of prayers all coming at him at once." (Here is one youngster who feels a little sorry for God and all His technical problems.) Yet, this young person finds the need for prayer. "Even not believing in Him as a superman, enthroned in Heaven, I still pray to Him on occasion, beginning: 'Oh, God, if there is a God, forgive me for doubting you.' "

Obviously, in our more sensitive and discerning young people, there is a genuine searching, a yearning to understand more about the meaning of life, of this universe, of our relationship with our fellow man, and with ultimate reality.

I feel tremendously gratified to find this impulse in our youth. I think they are somewhat startled, when they tell me that they no longer believe in God, to find that I react, not with reproachful anger, but with a kind of zestful enthusiasm: "Good," I tell them. "At least you are thinking about the problems of life. As long as there is a tentative quality in your voice, as long as you are not absolutely certain that what you have to say is eternal truth, we have something to talk about."

Why shouldn't a young person, alive to the facts of life, be raising real down-to-earth questions about the faith of his fathers? True, Moses told his people: "And God saw the light, that it was good; and God divided the light from the darkness. And God called the light Day; and the darkness He called Night." But Moses had never heard of Copernicus and Galileo.

What, then, are these words of Moses to us in the twentieth century? Are they the factual prose of cosmic history, or the fanciful poetry of a brilliant imagination?

And when the ancients wrote in the Bible that the waters under the Heaven were gathered together in one place, and "God called the dry land Earth," did they ever imagine that in 1962 an earthbound creature named John Glenn would fly around our planet with God-like speed, surveying in ninety minutes the whole universe conceived by the authors of our Bible? And Gagarin, another astronaut used the striking words of Genesis: "I saw the earth and it was very good." Could anyone, forty centuries ago, conceive of an Alan Shepard, who viewed the entire east coast of the United States from Maine to Florida in a few short minutes of suborbital flight?

Surely these are days when we are entitled to raise the most fundamental questions about our historic religion. On Yom Kippur, 1958, when Russia launched its first Sputnik, editorial writers in a number of Red capitals exclaimed exultantly: "Our Sputnik has just made a search of outer space and found no sign of God or the heaven He is supposed to inhabit."

Of course, when I look at a cosmic map, and realize that what our astronauts have seen so far is less than a speck on one galaxy among millions in this universe, I am still not ready to write off the Psalmist's declaration: "The Heavens de-

clare the Glory of God, and the firmament showeth His handiwork." Man may no longer be earthbound, but there is a good
deal of the cosmos he hasn't seen yet. One Cambridge University astronomer recently discovered new stars eight billion
light years away. The least the editor of *Pravda* should do, it
seems to me, is to wait until all the facts are in.

Nevertheless, I do not hesitate to tell my young friends:
"You need have no feelings of guilt in saying to yourself: 'I
can no longer accept the God of my ancient forefathers.'" It
is no sin to reject the idea of God as a superman.

Dr. Ira Eisenstein expresses this thought in a most illuminating way. "We have *conceptions* of God," he writes, "and
*beliefs* in God. Our conceptions change; our beliefs do not."
Obviously, our ideas about God cannot be the same as those
of Isaiah, or Rabbi Akiba, or Moses Mendelssohn. But because we realize, in a way that the prophets and the old rabbis
never could possibly comprehend, that this whole earth of
ours is less than a speck in the larger cosmos; that all the
chemicals that go to make up a man can be bought for less
than a dollar; that, according to the atomic physicists, if we
took away all the empty space in our bodies they would oc-
cupy less room than the head of a pin—does this mean that
we *believe* less than the most pious of our forefathers? Does
our greater knowledge about ourselves and the earth around
us prove to us that life has no meaning or purpose? Is the
rising of the sun on the water any less thrilling than it used
to be, or the cry of a newborn baby any less mysterious? Is
there any less magic in a young Anne Frank's haunting affirmation that, in spite of everything, men can be good, the air
can be clean, and there is hope for tomorrow? Our image of
God may have changed—but that doesn't mean we deny His
reality!

I have two ways of reacting whenever a young person tells
me he is an atheist. They depend mostly on the mood I'm in.
(We adults always react in one of two ways to teen-agers, if
I may betray a secret. There are some days when we are allergic to anything our teen-age children say or do. On such

days we should wear some kind of signal—a danger flag which says: Young man, or young lady, don't test us or yourself today. It's just not one of those days.)

When I'm not in a receptive frame of mind and a teen-ager tells me he's an atheist, I respond: "What colossal conceit! You don't know enough to qualify as an atheist. To be an atheist, you should at least be a philosopher and, according to Maimonides, you can't begin to be a philosopher until you have passed your thirtieth birthday and read everything you possibly can on the subject of history, philosophy, and religion. Giving yourself the title of atheist is like having calling cards printed with the words, 'Violin Virtuoso' or 'First-Class Scientist' under your name. It's a *chutzpah!*"

Fortunately, I am not often in that mood in the company of young people. So when a youngster tells me he is an atheist, I usually give him my triple test for atheism.

One, do you believe that all life is simply an accident . . . that we are born, live our years, and die without purpose, without meaning, without direction? Two, are you honestly convinced that there is nothing in this universe that is essentially good—that beauty isn't better than ugliness; unselfishness isn't better than self-seeking; truth isn't more precious than falsehood? And, finally, do you deny the possibility that man may some day, in some way—given his intelligence, given enlightenment, given education—create a more perfect society, with a minimum of hatred, and an ever-increasing mutual respect?

If life really has no meaning for you, if there are no values you cherish, if you really see man doomed to a perpetual jungle existence—then, and only then, are you an atheist.

Even Yuri Gagarin, child of the Communists, is probably not an atheist as he surveys the world from his space capsule. Consider, for example, the competition between his country and ours for the soul of Africa, the twentieth century's greatest prize. Americans and Russians both look upon the jungles of Africa, the peoples steeped in primitivism, and each country claims it has more to offer the Africans than its competitor.

But what does the competition consist of? Each is selling a different politico-economic system. Ours offers freedom, theirs does not. Yet the *product* we both offer is fundamentally the same. Both say, "We can help you build a decent world, with less disease, less misery, less ignorance, less bloodshed."

Even the so-called godless Soviets are saying there are values to be cherished and preserved—the human values of health, education, the arts, the sciences, all the decencies envisioned by the Hebrew prophets. I have heard some people say glibly that we of the West worship God and the Communists worship Man. But I am not as sure as I used to be about these distinctions. In a more serene future, even those who have abandoned religion in the name of science may some day come to a new and more exalted view of God.

In Irving Stone's biography of Michelangelo, *The Agony and the Ecstasy*, one of Michelangelo's friends threatens to report him as a heretic because he worships man. But the gifted artist, intoxicated as he is with the human form, replies: "No, I admire man, but I worship God for being able to create him." Surely, as we continue to marvel at the unending achievements of our modern scientists, we must think to ourselves: What a God to create such men!

So, when I talk with young people about their doubts and misgivings about God, I ask one favor—patience. Reserve judgment, I plead, about these basic problems of what to believe and what not to believe. We live in the midst of the most exciting era in human history. Scientists tell us that in one geophysical year more new knowledge was added to the sum total of known facts about our universe than were acquired in any previous *century* of man's existence. Obviously we are going to have to retool our religious instruments as well. Simple Orthodoxy, be it Christian or Jewish, just won't do.

Those who are impatient—as are some sixteen-year-olds in America, in Russia, and, if the truth be told, in Israel, too—who search the heavens as they move spiritually with the astronauts, hoping to find the God of Abraham, Isaac, and Jacob there, will lose faith. But those of us who cling tenaciously to the search for a God who is meaningful to modern man will be amply rewarded.

Science will provide us with the answers to many of life's mysteries; it will unlock doors to undreamed-of worlds. Some day our children may walk around the craters of the moon. Some day they may explore the Alps, the Himalayas, and the Andes on one quick twelve-hour tour on Columbus Day.

But never—and I mean *never*—will the major decisions of their lives be scientific decisions, as George Sarton has pointed out. Their relations with their parents, their choice of a career, the girls or boys they marry, the ethical code they establish for themselves—these are the decisions of a life well spent, and none of them will ever be expressed in a chemical formula, a mathematical equation, or a principle of physics.

If we master science, we will know a little more about the *true* and the *false* in life. But if we master religion, we have a more abiding knowledge of the *right* and the *wrong*. Science gives us *facts*. Faith gives us *values*—the values which lend meaning and dimension to human experience. That is why a scientist once said, "I never expect to understand most of the things I value most highly—the thrill of a sunset, a symphony, the love I have for certain persons."

Dr. Albert Einstein, the greatest scientist of our century and probably the greatest thinker of the past thousand years, left this reminder for all of us who are groping for truths we can never prove. He wrote: "The most beautiful emotion we can experience is the mystical . . . He to whom this emotion is a stranger, who can no longer wonder and stand rapt in awe, is as good as dead. To know that what is impenetrable to us really exists, manifesting itself as the highest wisdom and the most radiant beauty, which our dull faculties can comprehend only in their most primitive forms . . . this knowledge, this feeling is at the center of true religiousness."

What is infinite in man's life is not the distance he traverses, on earth or in the heavens, but his limitless reaching for that which is eternally true, eternally beautiful, and eternally good.

# Scientific Challenge and the Jewish Answer

WHAT IS CONSECRATION? It is a word related to holiness, to that which is sacred in life. Most of us are rather afraid of such words as sanctity, and we shy away from anything that suggests holiness. Yet, at some time in our lives most of us do experience a sense of holiness—though, ironically enough, it is usually away from a house of worship.

Whenever I fly over the Alps—and every time I travel to Europe I go out of my way to view the breathlessly beautiful snow-covered peaks—I am filled with a wondrous feeling of being near God's consecration. When a little baby discovers her toes for the first time, and her face lights up as Columbus's must have done when he sighted land—that, too, is a sacred moment. Often a glimpse of grandeur comes to us in the darkest hours of life. I once watched an old man, a sweet man nearing his ninetieth birthday, as he breathed his last breath. It was peaceful, quiet, and exquisitely triumphant. In that anguished moment of loss, we were overwhelmed by the sublime quality of his passing; we were conscious of the mystery in God's kiss of death.

We must not be embarrassed by the thought that holiness can be a vital ingredient of life's experience. Let us keep in mind, though, that the search for things holy should not be confined to official sanctuaries. (Sometimes that's the last place to look for them.)

A biology laboratory may suddenly open our eyes to the majestic orderliness in our universe. Even working out a

33

"beautiful" problem in mathematics sometimes results in a flashing glow of discovery. I know a boy genius who, at the age of eleven, understood enough advanced calculus to carry on a correspondence with some of the world's greatest mathematicians. His mother told me that one day when she called him away from his textbooks for supper he looked up and said: "Ah, Ma, just when I got to the most exciting part!" Young David, I am sure, as Eddington and Jeans and Einstein before him, often has caught a glimpse of holiness in the sublime world of mathematical perfection.

I dwell on this feeling of holiness, because it is another side to our worship of reason, an important argument for religion in a world enamored of science. It is good to be part of a faith that does not stress dogma—that does not list a series of beliefs in neat, inflexible fashion, and say to us: This you must believe or you are not a good and faithful follower. There are important historic reasons why Judaism has encouraged so much freedom of thought and action. We have come to regard ourselves not merely as a church, but as a *people*. And belonging to a *people* does not impose the same obligation to subscribe to a rigid set of doctrines or step out.

One great rabbi pictures heaven in a very concrete way, like the old rabbi in John Hersey's novel, *The Wall,* who shouted gaily to his fellow Jews before the firing squad: "Be happy, we are about to meet our Messiah." Another brilliant teacher declares, "The rabbis are not in heaven, but heaven is in the rabbis." Imagine a religion that has room for such different, conflicting ideas about what happens to us beyond the grave. That is Judaism.

Such a religion—not only Reform, but traditional Judaism as well—insists that man does not have all the answers. God doesn't change, it says to us over and over again, but our ideas about Him change. The more we know, the more we learn about His world. Science can only strengthen our Jewish faith.

There is a second aspect of Judaism which arms us in a unique way to meet the searching demands of this Age of

Science. Our tradition has stressed to an extraordinary degree, century after century, that we must develop the God-given brains with which we are endowed. The first requisite for Jewish hero status has been a high order of intelligence. There is an ancient saying in the *Ethics of the Fathers: Lo am ha-aretz chasid*—"An ignorant man cannot be a pious one." This is a radical statement, even for today. Think how much more radical it was 1,800 years ago.

A good Jew cannot be ignorant and religious at the same time. On the face of it, this notion seems hard to accept. Cannot a person who is uninformed, illiterate—let us say, a primitive man of the jungle—still have a genuine faith, an abiding awareness of God? The answer of Judaism is, No—and a very vigorous No, at that. The God of the Jews is not worshiped in unthinking fear or in blind love. We have insisted for three thousand years that reason is the handmaid of faith, that study and learning are indeed the highest forms of worship.

One of the most thrilling experiences, on a visit to the State of Israel, is to walk down any street in Tel Aviv and Jerusalem, and to see through the open windows the living rooms so clearly exposed. Do you know how you can tell that you are in a Jewish country? Every home, humble or affluent, has at least one wall lined with books. The song they sing in Israel on Shevuoth is *Yisroel, V'oraita chad hu*—"God, Israel, and Torah are one." In a very real sense, Jews and God and Learning are all one and the same.

There is a third exciting reason why our particular faith is matchlessly suited for the world we live in, and that is Judaism's insistence that religion is a way of living, rather than a way of talking. "Who is beloved of God," says our tradition, "is he who is beloved of man." If I want to find out whether a particular individual is a "good Jew" I look at the life he lives, at his relations with his family, his friends, his neighbors. Does he treat those who work for him with sensitivity and consideration? Does he handle his own job with conscientious integrity? Does he judge others—whatever their race or religion—purely on the basis of merit and human qualities? Does he share fully and wholeheartedly in the problems of his community?

There is a phrase we use traditionally, as we stand before the open Ark in the synagogue and prepare to accept the Torah: *Droche-ho darchey no-am*—"Its ways are ways of pleasantness." Life for a well-rounded and dedicated Jew is a life filled with infinite satisfactions of heart and mind, a life ever touched by God's presence and by the inward glow that comes to one who can say of himself: "I am truly a child of God. His ways are ways of pleasantness."

# Is Faith Obsolete?

EVERYONE WHO GIVES serious thought to his religion is conscious of the challenge of the physical sciences to our faith. No one can deny that there are important implications to our discovery that man is little more than a "nervous speck of stardust." I would suggest, however, that our religious convictions have been shaken less by what the physicist and the biochemist have told us about the nature of the *universe* than by what the psychologist, the anthropologist, and the sociologist have revealed to us about the nature of *man*.

From modern dynamic psychology we have learned much about the whys of human behavior. There are definable causes for a man's selfishness and, for that matter, his unselfishness. We know a good deal about neurotic behavior, about deviations from the normal. As a matter of fact, by the time young people finish high school these days, they have dipped deeply enough into the psychological sciences to begin wondering about the great saints of religion.

The dedicated men and women who lived utterly self-denying lives—were they mentally healthy people, or were they so filled with neurotic fears, repressed feelings, and the like that they are more to be pitied than praised? I am quite certain that if any child in our circle showed signs of becoming a saint, his parents would dispatch him by the speediest ambulance to the nearest child psychologist, to search out the causes of his abnormal behavior.

Other scientific disciplines—anthropology and comparative religion—also shatter some of the basic beliefs of classical religion. I remember, in my own college days, a class in comparative religion in which the professor pointed out that hundreds of years before the birth of Christianity, the founders of many of the great religions—Gautama the Buddha, Confucius, Osiris of Egypt—were considered by their followers to have come to earth in a miraculous virgin birth. One student, a girl, burst into tears and fled from the classroom. The professor had destroyed her faith!

It is the sociologist, however, who makes us wonder most about the truths we are taught in religious school. Take the distinction I often make, between the scientist who provides us with knowledge about what is true and what is false, and the religionist who helps us discriminate between right and wrong. "Ah no," says the social scientist, "we won't let you men of religion claim that area either." And he is quick to point out that the social history of mankind proves ideas of right and wrong to be highly relative. What is good? That which the overwhelming majority of people at one time, in one culture, in one region, regard as good. What is virtue in one culture may very well be a sin in another.

When I taught at the University of Iowa, in the School of Religion, we introduced a course on "Marriage and the Family." The head of the Sociology Department rushed to the dean in anguished protest. "How can you let that religious crowd teach a course in marriage? They are prejudiced in favor of monogamy!" A good social scientist would teach that some people favor a system of one wife per husband, and others have different moral standards. Who is right? Well, each group is right in its own eyes.

This notion that all truth is relative, a belief deeply rooted in our own American culture, has brought a number of blessings with it. We have become, by and large, a tolerant people, a live-and-let-live people in the realm of religion. The American creed of "my religion is good enough for me and your religion is good enough for you" has made life pleasanter in many ways. On the whole, we have respected the principle that a man's inner beliefs, his religious convictions, are his own private concern. The pied pipers of religious fanaticism have never been able to gather many followers.

But consider the price we have paid for accepting the idea that all truth—including religious truth—is relative. If there are no more absolute truths, no more insistent claims that this is what God wants, why behave according to moral rules?

In a great and respected university, a group of students were asked if they saw anything reprehensible in cheating on examinations. Forty per cent saw nothing wrong in the practice. In another poll, five out of six said they would participate in a rigged TV quiz program. At Columbia University, you may recall, students rose in righteous indignation in defense of Charles Van Doren: "He was only doing what any of us would do, if we could get away with it."

Again I ask, if there are no absolutes in life—nothing absolutely wrong and sinful, nothing categorically evil—why obey the moral law blindly?

I am not a Jeremiah who sees my generation skidding precipitously down the road to spiritual disaster. I am firmly convinced that this generation is as decent, as considerate, as filled with integrity, as any generation in the past. But I feel with every fiber of my being that if we continue to tolerate ethical shortcuts and moral short-changing, our society *will* ultimately destroy itself.

Most people think of science as dealing with the practical and religion as dealing with the ideal and the visionary. "Religion is a nice thing, but let's face it—you can't run the workaday world on it." Not long ago, a women's organization using the facilities of our temple invited a newspaperman to speak to them about America's relationship with Russia. After his lecture, one woman told me, in critical tones, "He sounded more like a rabbi than a newspaperman." (As though nothing could sound worse than a rabbi.)

One most persistent woman cornered the speaker on his way out of the auditorium: "What utter nonsense. What do you mean, love thy neighbor?" The speaker suggested that in a temple it was not altogether scandalous to mention the Golden Rule. She looked at him in incredulous contempt. "The very idea of a working journalist talking 'Shabbos language' in the middle of the week." Apparently, what we rabbis and ministers say from our pulpits is for the birds, not for people.

Perhaps it's our own fault that the people in the pews think of teachers of religion as part of a fantasy world. The prayers we recite together are too full of serenity, calm, and peacefulness.

Religion is not a substitute for phenobarbital—it's a prodding reminder about some of the basic facts of life. Yet, the so-called practical people are always astonished when we dreamy religionists make an accurate prediction.

The authorities in Albany, for example, seem very surprised that the bingo games conducted by some churches and synagogues have fallen into the control of criminal elements. An investigation is now under way—to my mind, a meaningless investigation. Yet, a long time ago, we on the New York Board of Rabbis, and in the Protestant Council, too, insisted that gambling was an immoral way to raise funds for religious institutions—that the practice would inevitably corrode and corrupt the very houses of God which sponsored it. It was the *practical* politicians who argued that people like to gamble and it was a good idea to put their weakness to good use. The so-called visionaries predicted with unerring accuracy that an unsanctified means ultimately destroys the most sacred of ends.

Religion should also have something to say in another arena of our scientific revolution—the challenge of automation. I agree with those forward-looking people who maintain that automation in industry, in transportation, in every aspect of our technology is here to stay. But I would insist that we put *human* engineering on the job as well.

Not long ago the New York City Transit System introduced an automatic train on one track of the shuttle service between Grand Central and Times Square. So we now have a train without an operator or conductor, a train that can go on endlessly, stopping, starting, doors opening and closing—all without direct human intervention. Perhaps the day will come when, instead of going into New York for a meeting, I can send an automaton who will answer to my name, ride on the automatic shuttle, and attend a meeting of other automatons, all programed to give the right electronic answers while we sit in the sun at the beach!

Seriously, the synagogue and the church must also be heard amidst the clamor of technical experts, eager to remake our society in a new image of engineering perfection. Granted that the world of photoelectrical eyes, microwaves, and satellite telecommunication is here to stay, we still have a responsibility to pause, take a deep breath, and ask what all this means in terms of human welfare. Is it good or bad for human beings? Does it enrich us, does it make people happier, does it truly enhance human experience? It is the job of religion ever to prod humanity with these searching questions.

I am convinced that our complex society, our modern scientific world, needs spiritual counsel and moral direction, *needs religion* more, not less, than the simple pastoral society of Biblical times. I think that the prophets were born 2,500 years too soon.

A few years ago, one of the most brilliant, most morally sensitive scientists of our age, Dr. J. Robert Oppenheimer, gave a university audience this description of modern man: "We know too much for one man to know much; we live too variously to live as one. Our knowledge separates us as well as it unites; our orders disintegrate as well as bind; our art brings us together and sets us apart. Diversity, complexity, richness overwhelm the man of today. Superficiality and fatigue become the temptations of those perpetually and precariously balanced between the infinitely open and the intimate. In such a time, each will have to cling to what is close to him, to what he knows, to what he can do, to his friends and his tradition, and his love, lest he be dissolved in universal confusion and know nothing and love nothing."

That's the gravest danger we face in our time—the ultimate discovery that we "know nothing and love nothing."

Soon after we dropped the bomb at Hiroshima, I had occasion to attend a conference at Reed College in Portland, Oregon. The meeting included a number of scientists, and the man I shared a room with was a famous atomic physicist. During the day this man was calm and composed, but at night I was awakened by the shrieks and groans of his terrifying nightmares. In the morning, I asked my roommate what troubled him so deeply. "I watched the first atom bomb bursting at Alamogordo," he told me. "I and my colleagues made that bomb, and I'm frightened. When I think of all the little-minded people there are in the world, I tremble. What will they do with our bomb? Will they have enough wisdom to keep it from obliterating mankind from the face of the globe? I'm a frightened man."

Science, as you see, does not have all the answers. And so I say to our young people: By all means acquire the skills necessary to be at home in the resplendent corridors of modern science. Follow your teacher's admonition to approach the world of knowledge with a proper scientific attitude. Be thorough; suspend judgment until you have all the facts; maintain a profound respect for truth.

But if life is to be more than a nightmare of uncertainty, more than a bewildering cry in the night, then seek, too, for answers to some of the larger questions: How can I as a human being find fulfillment in what I do? How can I, as a member of my society, add a little to its goodness, its warmth, its joy? Faith is no more obsolete in a world of science than man himself is superfluous.

At its best, science can only provide us with the tools to live a fuller life. A religious faith will continue to give our lives purpose and meaning.

# Love More

At the turn of the century, Sigmund Freud plucked a hitherto insignificant pronoun out of obscurity and elevated it to profound clinical importance. The concept of "self" that is wrapped up in the simple word "I," or Ego, explained Freud, is central to all of man's hopes and dreams, all of his feelings about everything that happens to him from his first breath to his last.

This insight into the structure of man's ego is, it should be recalled, deeply rooted in Jewish tradition. The Talmud, infinitely wise in psychological perception, declares: "Each human being should regard himself as though the world were created for his sake."

At first blush, what vanity this is—to view all of life as though its axis lay only in ourselves. Yet, there is a sobering sense of responsibility in this perspective. Man may say to himself: All that is in this wonderful world was created for my sake alone. I am king and master of everything my eyes behold and my senses feel—the loveliness of trees and stars and snowy landscape, the delicate fragrance of a garden of roses, the tingling touch of velvet, satisfying flavors; all the countless little pleasures of the senses—all the life forces of the universe—were designed for *my* sake, for the joys of *my* spirit. Surely one must live one's life in a way that justifies such inherent importance!

Martin Buber, another great pronoun exalter, augments Freud's emphasis on the "I" with his own compassionate reverence for the "thou," the intimate form of "you" in a number of languages, especially in the German and the Yiddish. And

Buber, whose unending search for meaningful relationships among men has made him a legend in his own lifetime, also dwells thoughtfully on the uniqueness of every man.

"God never does the same thing twice," writes Buber, quoting his favorite Hasidic rabbi, Nachman of Bratzlav. "It is because things happen but once that the individual partakes of eternity . . . Every man shall know and consider that in his qualities he is unique in the world and that none like him ever lived, for had there ever been someone like him, then he would not have needed to exist."

What a magnificent self-image: "I am absolutely special—so different that God took particular trouble to fashion me alone. *Not* one grain of salt in a shaker, *not* one pea in a pod. God has made me in an entirely different mold from anyone else."

Only when we accept the uniqueness within ourselves do we begin to understand the oneness of God—to gain a glimpse of God's image. And only when we feel secure in our own importance can we truly accept and respect the equal importance of others.

Martin Buber, in his incandescent book *I and Thou,* exhorts us to remember always that all other human beings are also special and unique.

Indeed, man is not man, declares Buber, unless he can relate fully to the people around him, identifying with their feelings, with their shortcomings, with all the strengths and weaknesses that make them human. It is this process of identification, this *getting inside* of another, that Buber considers *relating* on the level of *Thou.*

Buber goes much further—and now we move into the realm of his radical mysticism. Only by relating in an intimate way to another human being, he maintains, do we bring God into the world. God is incomplete, so to speak, without man. His very existence depends on man's ability to *relate*—to enter into the very being of his neighbor.

Why the word *Thou* and not the more common word *You? You* is impersonal, remote, detached. When a person says

*Thou,* he is saying: You and I are really two parts of the same process that produced us both, the same texture, the same quality, the same essence. That is why we say *Thou (Du)* to a brother or sister.

When we fall in love, the same spiritual chemistry takes place. We say *Thou* to the one we love. You and I are part and parcel of each other, we declare with this word. We are really one, psychologically, morally, spiritually.

In the same way, we Jews say *Thou* to our God, for we feel truly on intimate terms with Him. The Hasidim cultivated this notion of God as *du*—an uncapitalized *thou*. One of the best known Hasidic songs is "A Dudele," a constant repetition of the word in its diminutive: *du . . . du . . . du.* This same Hasidic motif is found in Paddy Chayevsky's *Gideon* in which the hero speaks so directly, on such a first-name basis with God. In response to the Angel's plea: "Will you not embrace me?" Gideon sighs: "It's not an easy thing to love you, God."

If we think of God as *thou*—and do we not every time we utter a blessing: *Baruch atah,* "Praised art Thou, O Lord"— we are really saying: I want to link myself with all of the cosmic process, to reach out with my very soul and say, I love thee, World; I love Thee, God; I want to be bound up with Thee!

Love is the key word in relating. Buber writes: "When a father complained to the Baal-Shem, 'My son is estranged from God—what shall I do?' he replied, 'Love him more.'"

Which is more important, Buber was asked, to love man, or to love God? And he answered, You can't have one without the other. When you reach out and say to your neighbor, "Thou art an integral part of my being," you clasp the hand of God.

Many of us in this antiseptic world of "reality" find Martin Buber's symbolic road to truth a complex path to follow. As prisoners of reason and rationality we cannot escape a feeling of envy toward those who, with such apparent ease, behold reality in another dimension. Buber extends his principle of *I and Thou* to all the world around him. He looks at a tree and imagines what it must be like to be a tree. He insists that children are much wiser than foolish adults who cannot see life in inanimate objects.

In his introduction to *Tales of the Hasidim,* Buber explains that his purpose is "to introduce the reader to a world of *legendary reality.*" The stories deal with what people saw, but the things they saw were apparent only to "the gaze of fervor." A reality born of fervor, but reality none the less, Buber insists, "unalloyed by invention and fantasy."

Of course, the fervor among Buber's followers is equal to that of the Hasidim he describes. I love the story Buber tells about himself, as a young professor. He had already won in his native Germany a reputation not only as a student of Hasidism but also, among the simple folk, as a Zaddik, a saintly leader able to help others to a clearer image of God.

As was his custom after a lecture, Dr. Buber had joined a few of his students in a coffee house for discussion. At the table he noticed a middle-aged Jew, rather modestly dressed, obviously wanting to engage him in conversation. After the students left, the timid soul summoned up courage and presented his problem:

"I'm a brother of your father's porter. You may not remember me, but I should like to ask you a question."

The young professor encouraged him: "I shall gladly give you whatever information I can."

"I have a daughter, and I also have a young man for my daughter. He is a student of law. He passed the examinations with distinction. Is he a steady man?"

The professor explained that although he did not know the man in question the description sounded as though he might be.

"But doctor, does he also have a good head?"

"That is even more difficult to answer," Buber answered hesitantly. "He must have something in his head."

"One final question: Doctor, should he now become a judge or a lawyer?"

Professor Buber pointed out that without knowing either

the daughter or her young man he was certainly in no position to pass judgment on the latter's vocational aptitudes.

"Ah, Doctor, you know. You just don't want to *say.*"

Every doctor, every clergyman, every public figure has been confronted by this same kind of sublime faith, this same conviction that, however remote or personal the problem, he as a leader knows the answer—even if, for some reason, he sees fit not to divulge it.

In an age so much better equipped with questions than answers, it must be comforting to feel there are some who do have all the answers. This is, I think, one of the essential appeals of Hasidism.

One final thought about Buber and his teachings. This is a man whose vision of God came ever so slowly and painfully. What stands out most in his autobiographical writings is the prodigious amount of contemplation that went into his ideas. So many of his insights lingered long behind clouds of confusion and uncertainty.

How often do our own ideas hover in our subconscious, never reaching the surface because we do not accord them the years of quiet contemplation, the long walks in the country, the countless hours of staring at the water's edge, the hilly horizon, the birds in flight.

Thus Buber teaches us not only a broader dimension of thought and belief, but also an invaluable lesson in *how* to think, *how* to believe, and *how* to see a vision of the universe.

# *How Far Social Relations?*

# How Far Social Relations?

AMERICAN JEWS live in a free society. Our community guarantees us freedom of movement, freedom of social contact with every other group, freedom to visit in any home which opens its doors to us, freedom to date and to marry anyone we choose.

But alongside this basic democratic value—our inalienable right to choose the life partner our heart desires—our particular group affirms an equally important value which we call group survival. And this, too, is an accepted value in this country.

It is part of the pride and glory of America that it blesses the continued existence of permanently distinguishable religious and cultural groups, be they Jews, Catholics, Mormons, or any others.

Here, however, is the paradox that faces us. What if one of these groups says to America: "We cannot survive as a group unless we put up certain social barriers that modify, and even contradict, the first democratic value—namely, the right of free contact in a free society." Does any group have the right to demand a double privilege—the privilege of social contact when and if it wants it, *and* the privilege of social separation when and if it wants that? I say the answer is yes. We Jews— and others as well—expect and have the right to expect the best of both worlds. Is there a contradiction in what we ask? Do we want to eat our democratic cake and still have it? Logically, perhaps, there *is* contradiction. But it is not an unreasonable inconsistency.

All Americans are first-class citizens—or hope to be. We are

constantly striving and moving toward that ideal. We interpret
our Constitution to guarantee us the choice of the occupation
we wish to follow, of the candidates we wish to elect, of the
community we wish to live in. And we fully expect that we
will be permitted to belong to any organized social group in
the community. If a luncheon club discriminates against Jews,
and some do, we insist that this is un-American. If a college
fraternity tells us that membership is restricted to followers of
a Christian church, that, too, we say, is un-American. If the
Scarsdale Country Club sets rules which bar members of the
Scarsdale Temple from its parties, we are quick to point out
that such actions fly in the face of the best American traditions.

Now, let us set this cherished democratic value alongside
of one we hold equally dear. I believe that we Jews, as a
group, have something precious to preserve. The Midrash, in
discussing the wonderful epic of Sinai—the giving of the Ten
Commandments to the children of Israel and, through them,
to the world—asks why God chose the wilderness of Sinai, so
remote, so forbidding, so desolate. The answer, say the rabbis,
is simple. God gave the Torah outside the Land of Israel to
symbolize the fact that the moral law was not meant for
Israel alone, but for all mankind. The Jews were chosen as
the instrument for conveying God's message to all.

Have these precepts been taken to heart, the principles of
justice, of compassion, of brotherhood? Look at the Congo;
look at Laos; look at the lands behind the Iron Curtain; look
at the cement jungles of our own land.

The world has much to learn, and I believe that we, the
descendants of those who stood at Sinai, have much to teach.
There is a very beautiful parable which says that not only the
people of Moses' generation stood at the foot of that mountain
when the Torah was given, but their children and their children's children. That means that you and I were there and
received our marching orders: Go and teach the world the
lessons of decency and truth.

What does all this mean to me as a parent? It means I have

an obligation to endow my own life with Jewish meaning and value. But it means even more: "Thou shalt teach them diligently unto thy children" are the first words which follow our affirmation of the *Shema.* I want the chain of tradition to remain unbroken. I want my children to fashion their homes with the symbols of Passover to remind them of the grandeur of liberty; with the pageantry of Hanukkah to remind them that the Maccabees held religious freedom more precious than life. I want for them the love of parent for child and child for parent that was the most distinguishing feature of their forefathers. I want a home where children learn by constant parental example their obligation to feed the hungry, give sight to the blind, and strengthen the weak and afflicted.

Cannot young people learn these values in a home not infused with Judaism? Of course they can. But it is infinitely easier in a household with a hundred generations of memories. If my great-grandparents loved music, cherished it and made their household resound with melody—and my grandparents and my parents as well—would it not be easy for me to instill that same love in my children? The biologists tell us that we don't transmit acquired characteristics. But surely much of what we make of ourselves is handed down to our children and grandchildren. I want to give my children, and to have them give their children, a Jewish home permeated with Jewish values.

If they marry outside of the faith, they will contribute to the disintegration and destruction of that exquisite goodness that is my faith. Yes, the non-Jewish partner may decide to cast his lot with ours; and those who have, in my experience, have succeeded in preserving, and often ennobling and enhancing, the chain of tradition.

But the harsh realities are against it. In 1933, the year Hitler seized power, over 28 per cent of German Jews married outside of their faith. Had Hitler not destroyed German Jewry, they would have succeeded in self-liquidation, as a recognizable group, virtually in our lifetime. In Budapest intermarriage ran as high as 60 per cent. It is not an accident that in those

communities where the rate of intermarriage is high, as in
Rome, for example, there is virtually no Jewish institutional
life, no training schools for religious teachers, no vital religious
activity.

What does all this mean concretely in Larchmont, Toledo,
Santa Barbara, Richmond, Oak Park, Durham, Houston, Ma-
maroneck? How are the parents of a sixteen-year-old in Westchester County involved in this large process of Jewish history?

By the time children are sixteen, they should have acquired
a certain feeling of historical continuity. They should sense
themselves as important links in an age-old chain. They may
still say to us one day, "Thanks, Dad; thanks, Mother; but I
have my own life to live, and who wants to mess around with
history?" But let's at least give them the live option. Let's let
them know that somehow they are related to the events at
Sinai; that somewhere in their historic past there is a tradition
that gave the world much of its cultivation; that the moral
code which makes the difference between barbarism and civilization had its roots in their blood stream. If they want to
resign, all right. *But let's give them the chance to know
what they are resigning from.*

Am I implying that if a Jewish boy has a date with a non-
Jewish girl, the course of history will be changed? Of course
not. But if that boy dates *only* gentile girls, or goes to a university where his choice is inevitably limited to non-Jewish
associations, he is in the process of divorcing himself from
Jewish values and Jewish ideals.

Let me be clearly understood. I do not want to ghettoize
Jewish children. I want them to mix freely, to work on high
school newspapers, to play on basketball teams, to dance with
young people of all races and creeds.

And after they are married, I would hope that their selec-
tion of friends will be unparochial, that their social life will
be much more rounded than that of their parents.

But—here is my inconsistency—during those crucial years
when permanent ties are cultivated, the ties that lead to mar-

riage, I would declare a kind of moratorium. I would ask
that boys and girls, young men and women, confine their
serious relationships at this time to those of their own faith.

Nor is this position exclusively a Jewish one. It is pro-
pounded with equal cogency by thoughtful Protestants and
Catholics. But we Jews are a minority and, as such, have a
far greater concern than the majority with the issue of survival.

There are undoubtedly many young people who would
come through still loyal to Jewish tradition and its values,
despite a large measure of interfaith dating. These youngsters
have so much self-respect and self-understanding as Jews that
they would not, under any circumstances, depart from the
ways of their forefathers. They love the beauties of Sabbath
and festival ceremonies; they have drunk deeply from the
wells of Jewish knowledge; and they have fallen permanently
in love with things Jewish.

According to the ancient *Ethics of the Fathers,* there are
two kinds of trees: those whose roots are shallow and easily
dislodged if a mighty wind blows across the field, and the
trees whose roots pierce so deeply into the earth that regardless of how fierce the gusts may be, they cannot be moved. I
would trust the boy or girl in my congregation who has read
and absorbed fifty good Jewish books; who has seen *Judgment
at Nuremberg* and *The Wall;* who has absorbed *Exodus* (with
all its blemishes) and *The Last of the Just;* who has taken
religious school seriously, and not merely marked time while
exposed to the great ideas and ideals of Judaism; who, most
significantly of all, has been reared in a home filled with love
and understanding of things Jewish—I would trust such a
person to date non-Jewish companions nine times out of ten
and nevertheless retain his Jewish integrity.

On the other hand, I question the wisdom of parents who
send their children to a college whose whole atmosphere is
uncongenial to Jewish values (I have in mind certain schools
in the South and Midwest, where traditions of some Christian
denominations are presented glamorously, while Judaism is
somehow downgraded). It is almost a miracle when such a

student returns with loyalties unimpaired and attachments to family traditions undisturbed.

What amazes me even more is the parent who has given his children no backbone whatever as Jews, whose home is indistinguishable from others in the way of family ceremonial or Jewish ideals, but who nevertheless fails to understand how his child could select a life-mate of another faith.

Some years ago, *The Christian Century* published an article entitled "When They're in Love, It's Too Late." It seems that life and love are quite unpredictable. But it has been my observation that, by and large, *most parents get the sons-in-law and daughters-in-law they deserve.* In the very process of nurturing our own children we are, to a considerable extent, nurturing our children-in-law, since we mold our youngsters to accept or reject certain kinds of people as their life-mates.

Am I a bigot? Am I demanding that the country club open its doors to me only for the privilege of my saying, "No, thanks"? I don't think so. America is big enough and strong enough to accommodate both those who want to lose their identity and uniqueness and those who want to preserve it; those who consider the public school the bedrock of our democracy, and those who find parochial schools the only solution; those who derive enough satisfaction and fulfillment in belonging to the dominant Protestant culture that is America, and those who would insist that America is enriched and blessed—that indeed all mankind is blessed—because we Jews would keep ourselves a bit apart: *in* America, *of* America, *for* America, and yet a little bit more than American alone.

# Intermarriage—
# What Chance for Success?

A NUMBER OF YEARS AGO two students came to see me in
my office at the University of Iowa. He was Protestant; she,
Catholic. The time: a few days before spring vacation. The
question: "Shall I bring my Protestant boy friend home to
spend Easter with my Catholic parents?" And, of course, the
ultimate query: "What are our chances for happiness?" "Well,"
I said to them, "you have the same chance for success as any
other students on campus—*if* you have no children; *if* neither
of you practices your own religion; *if* you live a thousand
miles away from either parental home."

When a man marries out of his faith, he has several adjust-
ments to make. The first is to accommodate himself to a person who does not share his ancestral beliefs. If he becomes a
father he must also live with children who are not Jews or
Protestants or Catholics, but some combination of these—let
us say, Jew-Catholic. The couple brings into the world a
child whose religious label is hazy, fuzzy, nondescript.

I wish I could describe clearly the feelings of so many
young people who have come to me out of this twilight atmosphere. The hybrid child, who is half Jew, half Christian, asks
himself in anguish of soul: How can one be half something,
half something else? How does one slice Judaism in half,
Protestantism down the middle? To belong to two faiths is like
belonging to two families: you belong nowhere.

But, you may ask, isn't the very genius of America that
quality we characterize as the free society? Anyone, at least in

the enlightened States, can marry anyone he chooses. Theoretically, that's true—and happily true. But also deeply in-
grained in America is what sociologists call the "triple melting
pot." Our neighbors think of us either as Protestants, as
Catholics, or as Jews. Yes, there's a little room for the religious abstainer, but he usually ends up with the label "non-
practicing Catholic" or "nonobservant Jew."

A young couple in the glowing flush of love finds it hard to
visualize problems that may not face them for twenty years.
But they come up, just the same. I told the two students seeking advice about a family who lived in a campus town. The
father was Jewish, inactive; the mother, Presbyterian and a
regular churchgoer. Their eighteen-year-old daughter was
"rushed" by a fashionable sorority and about to be pledged
when the shattering truth was revealed: Linda was Jewish! A
Jewish graduate of a Presbyterian Sunday school?

Linda was devastated by the heartless exclusion from the
sorority. Her mother, stricken with the excruciating torture of
seeing her child rejected, vented her wrath on her husband.
"Look what you've done to our poor, innocent Linda! You
with your miserable Jewishness!" The family ended up in the
divorce courts.

Perhaps religious neutrality is a desideratum in our society.
As a matter of fact, many thinking religionists long for the
days of the old-fashioned atheist . . . or at least the respectable
agnostic. For the very heart of religion lies in its being a matter of choice. I want my congregants to be Jews by choice, by
challenge, not by default. No self-respecting religious leader
wants congregants who follow out of habit, out of inertia, for
lack of something better to do.

But the hard facts of life in America today are that our
children in their school life, in their friendships, even later in
their business and professional life, will bear specific religious
labels—Catholic, Protestant, Jew. The religious shoe comes
in only three sizes, and woe unto the youngster who doesn't
fit into any of them.

You may well ask, Is comfort the only criterion for living?

My answer is found in the stubborn realities of life today, in the pervasive tensions which currently exist in American parent-child relations, in the constant tugs-of-war between parents unsure of their own authority and teen-agers searching for their unique place in the sun. Life is confused enough without the added complications of religious differences under one roof.

That is why I told my young friends that intermarriage which includes children is an invitation to disaster.

We come now to my second bit of advice to that young couple—the one about church or synagogue affiliation.

Of the 180 million Americans, 75 million belong to no church or synagogue. At first glance it should be no hardship to join the green pastures of those who pay no temple dues and fill no church collection plates. But here, too, the answer is far more involved than one would think. We may resign from a temple, or even refuse to join one. We can't resign from our ancestry.

From the cultural inheritance of our past, we derived an entire value system. For example, one of the hallmarks of a group is the way it treats its women, its wives and mothers. Not long ago, in an Algerian railway station, I saw a young husband sauntering into view, carrying nothing more than a cigarette case. His wife, aged about twenty-nine but looking sixty, walked behind him like a beast of burden, loaded down with a trunk and three suitcases. My value judgment was instantaneous: Here is a people not yet emerged from primitivism.

Part of the spiritual baggage we Jews carry with us all our lives, simply because we are Jews, is an attitude toward the partnership of husband and wife and toward family responsibility; it is a sensitivity for the feelings of our children, a whole complex of civilized insights into home life. I don't mean to suggest that all the Jewish men I know are ideal husbands and fathers. Some of them, in relation to their wives, seem never to have heard that Moses freed the slaves

3,500 years ago! But there *is* such a thing as a Jewish pattern of expectation in family relations.

Intermarriage, then, is something more than a casual choice of a life-mate whose religious address is different. *It is the establishment of a new home with a new character.*

I am not so blind or chauvinistic as to believe that there is grace and joy and charm only in a Jewish home. A Christian home worthy of the name has these ingredients, too. It is the home divorced from any religious tradition which terrifies me. Yet, in order to avoid religious strife, this is almost a requisite in intermarriages.

Now let's take a hard look at the school of thought that "love conquers all." After all, this argument goes, what difference does religion make? Joe can worship his God; Jane, hers. Aren't his God and hers one and the same Divinity? Don't both faiths teach essentially the same ideals?"

The ingenuousness, the naïveté of this argument rests on a very foggy understanding of what a specific religion is. A faith is not simply a credit card, enabling someone to shop at a particular church one day a week. A religion is a 365-day-a-year way of life.

Again, let me cite an actual example. A brilliant lawyer, Jewish, assistant attorney general of his state, asked my advice about his engagement to a Catholic girl. His Orthodox parents opposed the match. What did I think about their chances for happiness?

"Rabbi, she's a wonderful girl, sweet, well-educated; she got her master's degree at a Jesuit college."

"How will she feel about planned parenthood?" I asked.

"I don't know. But I'd let her do what she wants to about it."

Now I understood that when love conquers all, it sometimes vanquishes reason and common sense as well.

"How about the rest of her views," I asked. "How does she feel about censorship, about McCarthyism, about separation of Church and State? Does it really make no difference to you whether or not the person you plan to spend the rest of your life with shares your cherished convictions?"

Even the question of where I will spend eternity is at issue in an interfaith marriage. If my wife is Catholic, her answer will be different from mine. Is this a vital difference? I think it affects our entire life outlook.

The man who came to me was thirty-seven years old, well established, secure in many other facets of his life, yet facing the mystery of marriage as uncertainly as any young man does.

When a girl describes the dream man whose ring she wears by announcing that he dances marvelously, he's the life of every party, he bowls 220, I ask myself: What will he do when the baby wakes up for a 2 A.M. feeding, or the furnace goes off, or your mother says something indiscreet? How attentive and considerate will he be when you're sick . . . and when you're sixty?

Do any of us know what is in store for us an hour from now? One moment a couple stands before me as bride and groom; a few days later, they are scrambling for a life raft in the Atlantic while the *Andrea Doria* goes down. Every time I stand under a marriage canopy, I look straight into the eyes of the bride and groom and say: "All of us here are witnessing a tremendous act of faith. Two people stand here, soberly and solemnly, and declare: 'Of all the three billion people on the face of this globe, I have chosen just one to accompany me till my very last breath! In the person holding my hand lies *all* my fulfillment, *all* my hopes and dreams for happiness *every* day of my life!' " What a prodigious declaration of faith that is! No wonder Grandma's face, fashioned and chiseled by a half-century of marriage, is moist with tears.

I want the one who shares my child's life to share his thoughts, his moral and intellectual standards, and his life experiences. That's quite an assignment under the best of circumstances. Add to this the extra burden of a different religious tradition, and the chance of an ideal choice becomes infinitely more difficult.

My third injunction to the young student couple was: Live 1,000 miles away from either set of parents.

Most people simply cannot grasp the fact that one marries not only a person but a clan. The day a man gives his girl a ring he has chosen not only his bride, but his children's grandparents, uncles, aunts, cousins. He has determined where he will spend Christmas, Passover, perhaps even the summer vacations. He has made a decision, generally, between Hanukkah lights and Christmas trees, Yorkshire pudding and matzohball soup.

The young couple may share every view, and peace may prevail at the dinner table. But what of Uncle Patrick, who reads the *Brooklyn Tablet* piously and thinks the John Birch Society will save America from the Communists in the way Father Coughlin and Joe McCarthy tried to do before they were "crucified." And Cousin Tim, who is likely to remind Uncle Ben at a family get-together that if we aren't more vigilant the Rosenbergs and the Soblens will hand over America to the Russians without a shot fired.

You can see why I suggested to the young couple—it happened in Iowa—that they settle in Texas or Maine.

Do interfaith marriages ever work out well? Many of us know instances where they have. I myself have two friends, both mathematicians, living on a campus where faith lines are somewhat less rigid, half a continent away from parents, and without children. But whether there is a family or not, the indispensable ingredient is unity. It must be *one* home, *not two*; *one* set of values and ideals, *not two*; *one* focus of religious loyalty, *not two*.

One final word. There is a certain group responsibility each of us carries—particularly those of us whose group is a minority. Each time we make an important decision we must ask ourselves not only "What's in it for me?" but also "What does this decision mean to my group, to my people?"

I am concerned about the future of our Jewish tradition in America. I believe that Judaism has something priceless to offer our nation. Where will we get the national wisdom to steer a true course between the inexorable demands of military security, on the one hand, and cosmic annihilation on the other? Where will we find the moral stamina to resist civic corruption, family breakdown, ethical blindness? I see the answers in the traditional values of our prophets and sages. When we repeat the words of the Psalmist: "If God does not build a house, in vain do the builders toil," we're not just mouthing pretty words. We are enunciating principles as basic as the laws of Newton and Copernicus. A morally degenerate society contains within it the seeds of its own destruction. And destroy ourselves we will, unless we restore to the foundations of our society justice, decency, honesty, and truth.

I firmly believe that by making my home more Jewish, I perpetuate these life-sustaining values. I cherish the dream that America will always retain the Jewish element of its being as well as the Christain. That is why I dispute those who under the banner of the free society herald intermarriage as a keystone of democracy.

Some readers will think, "He says this because he's a rabbi." Actually, just the reverse is true. It's *because* I think this way that I am now a rabbi. And it is because I love both my Judaism and my America so dearly that I argue so strongly for a way of life that will preserve and cherish both.

# A New Day Dawning

JONATHAN SWIFT once wrote: "We have just enough religion to make us hate, but not enough to make us love one another." The history books, both ancient and modern, yield ample proof of that sage observation. But I'm prepared to accept the possibility that we are now embarking on a new stage of spiritual development. There are some heartening signs that, after almost nineteen centuries of sectarian strife, Western man may at last have decided it is possible to propagate his own faith without downgrading the religion of his neighbor.

Of course, some still say it can't be done. After all, they argue, if you are convinced that yours is the only true and straight path to God, do you not have to be equally convinced that all other signposts are misleading? Religious truth, these zealots maintain, is simply not a phrase which can be utilized in the plural.

Furthermore, the very interrelationship among the major Western faiths would seem to make conflict among them virtually inevitable. Christianity may be neutral where Buddhism or Hinduism are concerned, but it was conceived in Israel and dedicated to the proposition that Judaism encompasses only partial truth. "If I thought the religion of Jesus was no better than the religion of Moses, I would see no need for Christianity," declared one Protestant writer.

Just as Judaism developed out of a rejection of paganism, so Catholicism had its genesis in a rejection of Judaism: "*We*, not *they*, are the true Israel." And in the same way Protestantism is rooted in a disavowal of Catholicism. How then can any one of these faiths be expounded without invidious comparison? The very terms "Old Testament" and "New Testament" reflect a value judgment. A new machine is better than an old one; a new house more desirable than an antiquated one.

It is easy to see why, in the light of these bleak realities, those who dedicate themselves to the task of improving interfaith relations so often find their assignment overwhelming. There just seems to be no foreseeable end to the job.

It reminds me of the two synagogue sextons in a small Russian town who compared notes about their work.

"How much do you make, Mendel?"

"One hundred rubles a month. And you?"

"Twenty-five rubles."

"Twenty-five rubles! What kind of a living is that?"

"Well, I have just one duty to perform. Every morning I climb to the synagogue roof and look to see if the Messiah is coming. If I see him come riding down the street on his white horse, I'm supposed to rush down and summon the head of the synagogue."

"But only twenty-five rubles?" his friend challenged.

"Yes, I know it's not much of a job. But at least it's a lifetime proposition."

Certainly the job of creating interfaith harmony promises to be a "lifetime proposition." But where once I was quite pessimistic, I now have a good deal of hope about future Catholic-Jewish-Protestant relationships in America. There is a new day dawning, a day of "peaceful coexistence" among the different faiths.

What has determined the truce? I think that the answer lies in the monstrous tragedy of the Nazi extermination camps. True, the shedding of innocent blood has never shocked mankind for long. We have become inured to unjust suffering. But the unspeakable crimes of the Hitler era have, I am convinced, surpassed humanity's vast capacity to tolerate evil. Christianity, especially, found itself shaken to its very core by these events.

It is significant, I think, that Christian churchmen have not sought refuge in the argument that the Nazis were not Christian. A conscience that cannot be stilled asks: "Why, in a Christian country and in a Christian culture were millions of men, women, and children horribly put to death for no other reason than their descendancy from the stock that gave us our faith? Does the sin lie in us as individuals—or is it inherent in the very instruments of salvation we have fashioned?"

Christians are now beginning to realize how deeply their own teachings, their own interpretations—and more often misinterpretations—of their own theology have helped to fashion the bias they deplore. "The sad and shocking truth is," writes Bishop James A. Pike, of California, "that the roots of bias often reach back to the pulpit and the Sunday school class; the seeds of hatred frequently are planted by the churches themselves by what they *teach*, what they *fail to teach* and what they are."

All too often the lessons and sermons concerning the gentle Jesus are couched in language which arouses anything but gentleness. The Crucifixion story is, perhaps, most noteworthy in this regard. An Episcopalian bishop recounts the eye-opening experience of having a congregant come up at the end of a Good Friday service, muttering: "If I could just get my hands on a Jew now!"

And the two young Germans, a year ago in a Cologne courtroom, asked by the judge to explain why they had smeared swastikas on a synagogue, had among their other rantings the ready answer: "The Jews crucified our Lord."

Are these the ravings of warped minds who take the Oberammergau Passion Play too literally? Many sensitive Christians are no longer satisfied with this glib explanation. They are looking carefully at their own reflections—and are finding not the mirror but the original image seriously at fault.

One of the most promising areas of self-examination is that of religious education in the churches, the parochial schools, and the synagogues. In the past decade all three faiths have undertaken a critical analysis of the textbooks used in religious schools to see if, inadvertently, we have been teaching bigotry along with religion to the thirty-five million children who attend these classes. Yale Divinity School, St. Louis University, and Dropsie College have all had scholars investigating this question.

A pioneer in this field is Dr. Bernhard E. Olson, a Methodist minister who has dedicated his life to this problem. For his monumental study, *Faith and Prejudice,* just published, Dr. Olson studied over 120,000 Protestant lesson materials, utilizing all of our newly developed sociological measuring instruments in his appraisal. His findings were quite shocking—but they had the salutary effect of shocking a number of complacent people into action.

In recent years I attended two historic conferences of religious textbook editors and educators, one all-Protestant, and the other all-Catholic. They listened to candid reports about biased references in their own religious-school textbooks, and discussed without flinching their own shortcomings in permitting the perpetuation of old group libels and historical distortions.

No one was defensive. No one suggested, "Let the other fellow change his teachings about our group, and then we'll take care of our problem." Every educator, conservative and liberal, fundamentalist and modernist—and what an inspiration to see them all sitting together around a conference table in recognition that they were dealing with a common problem—agreed that as Americans and as Christians they had not only the responsibility to teach love in the abstract, but also the obligation to eliminate the kind of teaching that perpetuates hostilities born of centuries of conflict.

The overwhelming majority of men and women in religious affairs abhor prejudice. Dedicated though they are to the transmission of a specific heritage, they will not knowingly purchase loyalty to their faith at the price of bigotry. Show a religious textbook writer or editor how his own material is likely to evoke negative stereotypes, and he will recoil with dismay at his own short-sightedness.

One Protestant educator expressed his agony of conscience in this searing challenge to some of his colleagues: "The man who pressed the button in the Nazi gas chambers—where was he at 11 A.M. on a Sunday morning, when he was eleven years old? What image of Jews did he carry away as he left the Sunday school classroom, which enabled him, years later, to blot out the lives of Jews without wincing at the thought that these were human beings like himself? Or had he somehow been persuaded, by virtue of his religious training, that they were something less than human?"

Several divinity school professors who had supervised a critical analysis of Sunday school textbooks were deeply moved by the forthrightness of the editors and their willingness to point the finger of accusation at themselves. They felt, one professor declared, that they were part of "a theological revolution." For nineteen centuries religionists had accepted as normal the bitter consequences of controversy. Even the noblest-minded among them never faced up to the consequences of presenting religious doctrines in such a way as to divide mankind into heroes and villains. Now, modern religious-school textbook editors are examining their work with this added criterion: Will it cultivate respect for those outside our fold as well as for our own people?

Certainly religious isolationism and chauvinism are far from dead. But we have come a long way since each religious group in America was an island unto itself. Late in 1961 the national convention of the Catholic Interracial Council, whose spiritual mentor is Father John La Farge, urged local Councils "to arrange visits to Jewish synagogues for Catholic adults and young persons." The Council also encouraged "visits to local Jewish spokesmen for our Catholic eighth-grade and high-school students, to answer questions and explain Jewish beliefs."

Protestant leaders, too, are helping their children and

young adults to understand the values of Judaism, the meaning of Jewish celebrations, the many areas of common heritage they share with Jews.

We are much too close to recent religious events to measure their impact on future generations. A papal pronouncement, a declaration by the World Council of Churches, condemning anti-Semitism may seem somewhat starry-eyed, but I discern in all of these developments a gigantic step forward in Christian-Jewish relations.

When Pope John XXIII ordered the elimination of the anti-Jewish tone in the Easter liturgy, the American diocesan newspapers heralded the changes in very significant headlines: "Pope Orders Removal of Anti-Jewish Texts . . . Out of Respect for Other Faiths." The historic words "other faiths" underscore a new awareness of the pluralistic nature of the religious world.

And the land most devastatingly convulsed by anti-Semitism —Germany—has also recently heard its Lutheran bishops proclaim its grief and guilt: Why did we fail humanity? How can the German Church atone for its sins? "Our people must try everything humanly possible to make amends for the injustices done to the Jewish people and to other peoples." Their words find an eloquent echo in the official newspaper of the Vatican, *Osservatore Romano,* whose editor, Raimondo Manzini, wrote in August, 1961, in reaction to the Eichmann trial: "Humanity today seems to be looking at itself in the mirror of its past errors to convince itself that it has been capable of such crimes against God. . . . Let us therefore re-think, re-live, remember things."

Retracing the long upward road we have traversed in interfaith relationships in the past decade, I am less daunted by the precipitous ascent that lies ahead. The job may still be "a lifetime proposition." But though the Messiah is still some distance away from Main Street, there are some sounds that may prove to be his footsteps not too far away.

# The Travels of Jonah

MY FAVORITE Biblical personality has no name. He wrote one of the books of the Bible, but preferred to remain anonymous. We know nothing about the author of the Book of Jonah as an individual. But we do know he had a delightful self-effacing humor that continues to endear him to his readers.

Perhaps when Jonah's creator first wrote the story of the prophet and the whale, some of his contemporaries knew his identity, but most people probably did not; just as few people in Jonathan Swift's day knew that the Gulliver who recorded his fabulous travels was really the Dean of Dublin's St. Patrick's Cathedral. Gulliver, too, was written anonymously; Swift's authorship was revealed only after his death, some two decades after the book was first published.

There is an intriguing similarity between Jonah and Gulliver. Both characters were so colorful and captivating, their experiences so bedazzling, that the deeper messages behind their stories often were lost in the adventures. It is not surprising that, over the centuries, both tales became designated as children's stories rather than the sophisticated adult morality plays they were intended to be. Both authors were, perhaps, just a bit too subtle and far advanced for their time.

Take, for example, the question of heroes and villains. Traditionally, the villain wears the robe of the stranger, while the hero is drawn to resemble "the folks at home." Since people see in drama a projection of themselves, it must be a happy projection. Thus, when Shakespeare read an Italian story about a Christian merchant who demanded a pound of flesh from a Jew, he reversed these roles in his own *Merchant of Venice*. He would have been hissed off the Elizabethan stage if he had left the original tale intact.

Now examine the story of Jonah. Every decent person in the Biblical tale—the sympathetic sailors, the gallant captain, the remorseful Assyrians—all are gentiles. The only questionable character in the entire tale, as Professor Sheldon Blank points out in a brillant essay, is the spineless Jonah, the Hebrew. Why, then, did the Jews love that story, take it to their hearts, incorporate it into the ritual of the year's holiest day, Yom Kippur?

Part of the answer lies in the fact that it is a masterful tale. But the rabbis who introduced it into the liturgy were more impressed with its ethical grandeur than its unforgettable story. For Jonah's conflicts underscore the Jewish teaching that God is concerned with *all* his creatures, regardless of their tribal label.

There is a subtle irony in the final chapter of this little book. Jonah has been asked to preach to the Assyrians, the Nazis of those days. Not much of an assignment for a nice Jewish prophet. Having little stomach for the mission, he books passage for distant Tarshish, assuming that once he has left Palestine he is beyond God's jurisdiction. (Every time I stand at the port of modern Jaffa, I see the breathless Jonah paying his fare, as the Bible describes it, and asking the captain to give him a one-way ticket to anywhere.)

Of course we know the denouement. Jonah discovers that God's domain extends far beyond Israel, a fact that the unlearned, heathen sailors knew well. In fact, every unlettered person in the story seems to be better informed than the official prophet.

Finally, the unwilling Jonah preaches that only a penitent Nineveh can be saved. The Assyrians repent, and they are saved. But Jonah is miserable: his prophecy has surprisingly come true, but he can't really believe it himself.

The author of Jonah, then, is a charmingly mature person. He can laugh at himself and find amusement even in the sacred profession of prophecy. And with this laughter he reminds his fellow Jews not to take themselves too seriously, even as God's chosen people. For this nameless storyteller the Mosaic injunction "love of stranger" lay at the very heart of the Hebraic spirit. He sought to give his compatriots a vision of God that was universal, embodying one vast brotherhood. Today, twenty-five centuries later, this lesson has still not taken root.

If modern man had that ancient writer's sophistication, no moment would be wasted on the fruitless debate about whether a human being could survive Jonah's incarceration. Instead, we would ponder the vivid symbols in the Biblical narrative and ask ourselves: What was this genius of ancient Israel trying to teach us about the still-unattained brotherhood of man?

# The Texture of Life

I ALWAYS LOOK FORWARD with excitement to the High Holy Day season. There is a special, inexpressible quality about Rosh Hashanah and Yom Kippur that makes me feel different inwardly.

First of all, in our part of the world and our particular American rhythm, it is a season of beginning. Families are reunited after summer at camp or travel. Some of our children start kindergarten for the first time, others, junior high and high school, still others, college. We don our new clothes and, even more important, the new mantle of optimism that comes to most people at the start of a new season, and we say to ourselves: Perhaps this year will be much better than last.

This mood is enhanced by the lovely tradition which declares *Hayom Harat Olam*, "Today is the world's birthday." According to ancient rabbinic tradition, creation began not in January or June, but in September. Adam and Eve entered the Garden of Eden in September. Who knows what paradise awaits us this month?

Many of us grew up in an environment where, on Rosh Hashanah, the very air we breathed, the atmosphere of the streets, the tempo of the neighborhood, the heartbeat of the world around us, was exquisitely different. Remember the way people walked leisurely, with measured pace on certain favorite streets? There were certain streets—upper Seventh Avenue, or West End Avenue, or Ocean Avenue, or Douglas Boulevard (in my home town it was College Street)—where you knew you would pass all of your friends walking the other way. Cheerful greetings of "Happy New Year" filled the air. It was a day whose joy you could almost touch. So

Rosh Hashanah seemed like a dearly loved relative who lived far away and had wired he was on his way to visit, and you couldn't wait to see his face again.

Do you know that ancient Jews felt that way about every "ordinary" Sabbath? Why is it required by Jewish law that we eat an extra meal on the Sabbath? Because on that day, in a mystical way, all Jews are endowed with a *Neshama Yeserah* —"an extra soul." We are two people on the Sabbath: our regular selves and our special selves. Both have to be fed and, indeed, each deserves a little *challah* (bread).

What a profound insight this is, that each of us is not just one person, but two: our everyday, workaday, mundane selves, bogged down in our jobs and our basic needs; and our very special selves, that seek only the better, more permanent, more enduring things in life—the angel within us, the God within us.

Maybe that's why, on Rosh Hashanah, it's traditional as we sit at the dinner table, to dip our bread in honey and pray that the year be sweet and good to us! It is of the better "us," the special soul within us that we talk about.

But of course this is also a time of the year when we review in our minds the months that have passed. A rabbi in the midst of the twentieth century, working among people who refuse to assume that whatever was good enough for their grandfathers is good enough for them, and whose traditions cannot be sanctified by time alone, must be prepared to face some pretty searching questions.

The biggest question, spoken or unspoken, is: Why religion? Why Judaism? In what way is it indispensable in my life? Especially if I am quite young and still seeking to fashion my life in a meaningful way. Do I really need religion? Not long ago, at a wedding party, a college student said to me: "Haven't you noticed, Rabbi, that we college people no longer find the need for religion?"

The answer to that question, for me, lies in what I think of as the texture of life.

There are several ways of examining a piece of cloth. When

you study it from a distance as, for example, those who sit near the rear of the sanctuary survey the hangings up front, it is almost impossible to discern whether the fabric is fine or coarse. It is only when you approach closely and feel the texture that you can judge whether the material is woven with fine threads, if there are skimpy strands in the fabric, if the man who fashioned it wanted it sheer or opaque.

So, too, with a human being. Viewed from a distance, one life is lived very much like another. But if you come closer, if you begin to examine the different patterns of living as you do, for example, in some penetrating biographies, you begin to gather something about each life's unique quality. That's why reading an excellent biography is such a rewarding experience. For through it we approach another human being, be it Disraeli, or Michelangelo, or John F. Kennedy, in an intimate dimension. Those who enjoyed, as I did, *The Making of the President, 1960,* must have shared my initial feeling: What is there in this book, I asked myself, that a faithful reader of the *New York Times* doesn't already know about Kennedy's election campaign? Yet it is a glimpse at this very quality I'm discussing, the rich, thickly woven texture of life, that makes this book a gem.

A true religious experience—and by religious experience I don't mean a casual, once-in-a-lifetime contact, but a day-by-day reverence toward the wonder of life—enriches the texture of every life it touches.

Last summer we spent some time on a farm south of Tel Aviv, operated by a cousin of mine. The lovely orchards in the rolling country where Samson had fought the Philistines were filled with oranges, grapefruit, olives, grapes, bananas, almonds, and walnuts. The earth was generous of its bounty, responsive to the loving nurture of people who had lived intimately with the soil for generations. My cousin's name is Abraham, after the very first Hebrew who came from distant Chaldea to plow this land. Abraham asked my sons, David and Jonathan, if they had ever watched bees making honey. He showed us how clannish bees are. If a visiting bee does not belong to the family, the rest of the *mishpochah* pushes him out of the hive . . . unless he happens to have some honey on him, in which case he is admitted.

Abraham said to us: "Do you remember, the Bible said that some day God would make of this place a land flowing with milk and honey? Just think, that bee working so diligently is helping God to keep His promise."

There are two ways to look at a bee. One is to see him as an insect, dangerous, threatening, something to flee from. Another is to see him as a servant of the Lord, carrying his offering of honey in accordance with God's will. Abraham's life, seemingly that of a prosaic farmer, has this wonderful dimension of divine meaning.

What does the phrase "atomic energy" mean to you? An atomic missile on a launching pad in the Urals, labeled "Destination U.S.A."? Or a breathless sense of mystery, an awe about the ability to manipulate invisible matter and release undreamt-of energy for the good of all humanity? Disaster or a growing achievement for all mankind?

A few months ago, I stood in the British Museum and gazed at a Greek statue sculptured in 1400 B.C.E. The marble still glowed; the figure still balanced with perfect grace after more than 3,000 years. No one knows the name of the sculptor who speaks to us across the millennia, but his creative genius touches all who see his work. How much more glorious, then, is the intricate design of this universe we inhabit. Does it not impel us to think: What an architect, what an artist lies behind all of creation!

When I look at life through religious eyes, I see my fellow man in a broader perspective. Two human beings at a distance look exactly alike. But when I draw closer I can see that one of them is a derelict, a frustration to himself and an anguish to those who love him, while another—let's say his name is Learned Hand—has devoted a life span of nine decades to every refreshing attribute of heart and mind. One man is a failure; the other a human being as God wanted a human being to turn out—an infinite source of stimulation and joy to himself and to others.

What is the difference between a religious perspective on life and its opposite? The answer may well lie in the philosophy of a certain woman I have come to know. She is the principal of a girls' school in Jerusalem, a deeply devout woman in her fifties, born in Israel. Her students are all Oriental children, some from Iraq, some from Morocco, most of them dark-skinned children of Kurdish Jews, from the hills of far-off Persia.

If you and I were to look at these children and their parents, if we were to visit their homes as she does, what would we see? Primitives who have never used a toothbrush in their lives, whose hair until recently had never known a comb, who never sat on a chair or near a table until they were transported to Jerusalem. All of this is true . . . but that isn't what Abigail sees.

On my last visit to Israel she pointed to these dark-skinned children and said: "Have you ever seen such potentiality in your life? What good-natured people! How eager they are to lift themselves by their bootstraps! What wonderful human beings they will *become* if we give them our love and show them that we care." In Abigail's eyes, it is what a person *can become* that counts. Through the eyes of faith she sees beneath the dust on their cheeks what their God-given souls must look like. And they fulfill her expectation of them.

Still another strand in the texture of life marks the religious person. That strand is purpose or direction. There is a lovely legend of the rabbis, telling of a bargain God had struck with man. God says: "I will make a deal with you. I will keep the sun in the skies, the seasons in their places, the earth's fruit in order. Just watch; each day the sun will rise at its appointed station; the winds will bring rain in the spring; and every time you drop a seed in the soil, the right flower will sprout. Now you, Man, you go about your business in the same orderly fashion, living life as it should be lived!"

The human being who says to himself, "I am *not* a mere accident of physical existence," who is truly convinced that his sojourn on this earth has meaning and purpose, and that in the divine order of things what he does in life really matters—that person cannot find life boring. He has no time for brooding or self-pity because there are not enough hours in the day to finish all he wants to do; because what he calls his *self* and what he sees as his *goal* and *purpose* in life are bound together as one.

Essentially, this is the meaning of Rosh Hashanah. It is the time of year when the individual worshiper stops asking the rabbi, How can I cultivate a religious feeling within me? and asks himself instead: Where are the resources within me . . . what books shall I read; what company shall I seek; how much time for contemplation or quiet meditation shall I allot in the coming months to help me feel the texture of life?

In our prayer book, we read *Avinu Malkeinu* . . . "Our Father our King, inscribe us in the Book of Life." The Hebrew reads *Chayim Tovim,* not just "life," but the "*good* life" . . . a life textured with purpose and dedicated to acts that add beauty and grace, elevation of mind and nobility of spirit in our journey through this world.

# Tenderness—
# Prescription for Survival

ON THE DAY that U-2 pilot Francis Gary Powers was liberated by the Russians in a dramatic exchange for their own Rudolph Abel, I was seated at dinner with a couple, both intelligent and kindly disposed, who spoke very bitterly about the U-2 returnee.

"He violated his contract," they insisted. "It was part of his agreement with the United States Government that he would commit suicide rather than fall into Russian hands!"

Of course, none of us had any information to support this widespread report about the pilot's contractual arrangements with his employers—in this instance, the American people. But we discussed the question abstractly, none the less. If a man is generously compensated for a risky undertaking, doesn't he have an obligation to live up to his commitment?

To me there is a pagan quality to such reasoning. A man may choose—as countless have chosen in glorious pages of history—to die for a cause he cherishes more than life itself. But can one really *buy* the life of a human being? We pay a test pilot for *risking* his life, yes. But my religion teaches that human life is so precious it cannot be bartered. Thus, any contract setting deliberate self-destruction as one of its conditions is immoral and obscene.

What has happened to our moral perspective that these two decent people, and so many others like them, can think so callously—can view the human soul so lightly? A great many people are horrified at the thought that a doctor, moved

79

by compassion, might be tempted to speed the end for a patient tortured by a hopeless malignancy. Yet when reports of the so-called Powers contract were published, there was no indignation at all at the possibility that our Government had exacted such an inhuman commitment.

Surely it behooves all those self-righteous souls in and out of government who demand to know why Mr. Powers didn't inject himself with the poison at least to cough with embarrassment when they ask the question. Or have we gotten so tough that we don't even find the question embarrassing?

We live in an age that venerates toughness—often for its own sake. Two acrobats slip to their deaths from the high wires during a circus performance, and there is momentary shock. But the rest of the troupe bravely announces its determination to carry on, and "The show must go on"—but must it, really? And if it does, must it continue to go on without lifesaving nets below the wire, just to provide the audience with that extra added thrill? A racing car lurches out of control on the track and snuffs out the lives of a score of bystanders. There are some feelings of revulsion and horror, it's true, but they are never enough to interfere with the next year's races. Every four years, a hundred young men die on the battlefields of football, but there is no real pressure for those safety measures which would avoid such slaughter. Death, it seems, is a price modern man is willing to pay for exciting entertainment.

And what toughness we can muster in the name of progress. A giant bulldozer makes way for a new superhighway, crushing aside all the houses that stand in its path. For the dispossessed families, a lifetime of memories are buried with the rubble. But what are a few precious memories compared to a four-lane throughway?

I'm beginning to wonder what public referendum decided to abolish the age of tenderness and inaugurate the era of toughness instead. Does anyone remember when we repealed the constitution of compassion and voted to set in motion the process of dehumanization?

This toughness we exalt contains three basic ingredients. First, we persuade ourselves that the goals we have set are so sacred that any means we employ to achieve them are justified. (There is a nagging recognition that such a claim is not original with us—and that we have been unwilling to accept it from its original source. But it's different for us, we tell ourselves, because *our* goals are so honorable and "theirs" are not.) In the name of *our* goal of national survival, we permit some of our fellow Americans to be deprived of their civil liberties because they will not betray the friends of their youth on the witness stand. We squirm with momentary moral discomfort while we watch our Government engage in this sordid business in our name, but then we still our conscience and readjust our ethical barometer. Ironically, the very people who clamor loudest that they would rather be "dead than Red," implying, at least, that there are values—decency, truth, integrity—more cherished than life itself, evince few scruples about doing violence to these values for the sake of what Maurice Samuel once described as "an obsession with survival."

Efficiency as an end in itself is a second component of our toughness. "Survival of the fittest" has been transmuted from a biological thesis into a worthwhile ideal. Life is a game that all of us are expected to play—and "good players" are respected, win, lose, or draw. General Rommel was a Nazi whose goal was to destroy British and American lives for the glory of Hitler, but we pay breathless tribute to his inordinate skill. A U-boat commander whose torpedoes sent thousands of young Americans to watery graves during World War II is feted at a luncheon club a dozen years later. The Germans butchered millions of innocent men, women, and children, but they were so *efficient* at it. And Mussolini *did* make those Italian trains run on time. Skill deserves respect, we say— even the skill directed to the annihilation of the boy next door.

Finally, the third basic ingredient in toughness is the principle that the individual must always yield to the group—"The greatest good of the greatest number." That's why we feel no compunction about asking a family to abandon its home for the sake of a new road. For personal feelings, grief, nostalgia, pangs of separation—all are irrelevant to the needs of society.

Who can deny that risks and progress are necessary, that the old must often give way to the new? But not everything new is synonymous with progress. Sometimes I ponder over a mathematical formula which multiplies the number of unnecessary trips I have taken over the new highway near my home by the number of my fellow Americans utilizing the same road, and the figure I arrive at is staggering. There was a slogan popular during World War II that we might well paraphrase: Is this change—or this risk—really necessary?

Those of us who advocate tenderness as one of our life goals are not unmindful of all the complexities of modern living that make this goal difficult to achieve. Gone are the idyllic days—if they ever really existed—when ethical decisions could be made without all the cluttering political, economic, and socio-ethnic factors that come into play today. But none of these factors absolve us—any one of us—from our individual responsibility to deal with our fellow human beings *as* human beings, and not as impersonal cogs in some highly efficient machine. Machines must be perfect—or they get scrapped. Human beings are *not* perfect, and it is their job to accept, to understand, and to forgive each other's imperfections—not only as a Sabbath exercise once a week, but as a way of life.

My friends who had so indignantly demanded suicide of Mr. Powers were not at all surprised when I disagreed with them.

"Of course, Rabbi, you're a man of God. We expect *you* to be tender-hearted."

Well, I expect the rest of us to be tender-hearted too. And I advocate it as the last best hope of a world that has followed the path of toughness to the very brink of self-destruction.

Tenderness is not weakness, not softness, not self-effacement. Tenderness is a way of life which insists that we must use good and decent means for good ends; that cherishes co-operation above competition; that is based in the recognition that every single human being is precious in God's sight.

If we extend our own range of tenderness to encompass all those whose lives touch ours; if we refuse steadfastly to accept evil as an expediency and inhumanity as a temporary necessity—only then can we hope to find the satisfaction and purpose so often missing in our restless lives.

# Jews and the Public Schools

MARY ANTIN in her wonderful testament to America, *The Promised Land*, describes the awe with which her father first brought his young daughter to the public school in Boston: In the eyes of this parent, the woman who was to teach his child represented America at its very best—an embodiment of all the hopes and dreams that had brought him to the New World.

The same adulation of the public school is to be found in virtually every sketch of first-generation Jewish life; indeed the promise of a free secular education for their children was one of the strongest forces pulling Jewish immigrants toward America. It is not hard to understand our parents' tremendous emotional investment in the public schools, nor the present generation's continued efforts to preserve their special qualities. For many years the school was the immigrant Jew's sole contact with the State. Before the days of income taxes, social security, and public-welfare agencies, the struggling, law-abiding new American seldom had any dealings with the various arms of government. Among the dreams for tomorrow, American citizenship was, of course, a very special goal—and this too was to be attained through night-school classes at the public school.

The Jews of Eastern Europe, who constituted the overwhelming majority of all Jewish immigrants, had never before tasted the fruits of first-class citizenship. Here for the first time in almost two millennia a Jewish community took root in a religiously *neutral* country, a land which Jefferson and Madison and their colleagues had made impartial in matters of

faith. Little wonder that during the ten to fifteen years following 1915, when this country experienced a reverse migra-
tion trend and 56 per cent of the newly arrived immigrants
returned to Europe, only 4 per cent of the Jews went back.

Given this image of the public school as a reflection of
America at its best, that is, strictly impartial in matters of
religion, we can more readily understand American Jewry's
resistance to any sectarian intrusion into public education. A
long and bitter history has taught us that the State cannot
take an "impartial hand" in religious affairs.

But why should Jews oppose a practice such as "released
time," which enables students to leave their public school
classroom an hour early once a week to attend church or
synagogue classes, I am asked. Don't Jews want their children
to be religiously literate? Of course we do. The annual budget
of the American Jewish community for religious instruction
amounts to over $100 per child. We are very eager to see our
youngsters in our religious schools, but we do *not* want the
public school to send them there. The very thought of a
teacher calling on the Catholic children to march in one line,
the Protestants in a second, and the Jews in a third conjures up
in our minds all the nightmares of the Polish ghetto.

I have heard some Christian advocates of released time
say we Jews are inconsistent: Don't we keep our children out
of school on the High Holy Days? Doesn't this kind of separation also dramatize differences? But it isn't a fear of difference that concerns us. No one is suggesting that children—or
their parents—hide their faith. It is the notion, rather, that
the State—in this case, that arm of the State which is the
school—makes these faith distinctions that is anathema to
Jewish parents.

That's all very well, argue the proponents of more religion
in the schools. But why do Jews always line up with the non-
believers in opposing programs to strengthen the moral character of the children? What's wrong with the public schools
teaching belief in God? How simple that sounds—as though

centuries of bloodshed over how belief in God should be
taught had never occurred!

We Jews have never believed that religion is bound up
with *words*. We have little faith in the efficacy of verbaliza-
tion. The repetition of the commandment *Thou shalt not steal*
will not, we feel, move man one millimeter closer to integrity.
Nor can we see any value in posting the Ten Commandments
in the classroom, as advocated by some well-intentioned citizens in New Hyde Park, New York. As it happens we've had
quite a history in connection with the symbolic use of the Ten
Commandments. As students of Jewish history know, the
Decalogue originally was incorporated into the liturgy of the
ancient Temple in Jerusalem. But over the years the commandments became objects of special veneration and the
ancient rabbis, with typical Jewish allergy to making idols
even when sacred symbols were involved, eliminated them
from the worship service. Now, almost two thousand years
later, a local Board of Education wants to undo their work!

Our opposition to the reading of the Old Testament in
public-school classes also puzzles many people. Why shouldn't
a child learn to embrace the 23rd Psalm just as he does a
Wordsworth sonnet? I would agree that a sound knowledge
of the Bible ought to be part of the intellectual equipment
of every informed human being. Indeed I am convinced it is
impossible to understand our culture and its literature without
it. But I must distinguish sharply between Bible reading as an
act of worship and the reading of a Biblical passage in the
context of learning. I believe that requiring a teacher to read
ten verses of the Bible every morning without comment is
both bad religion and bad pedagogy. I love the words of
Amos and Micah too much to have them handled without
tender care.

In the same way, a Jew takes no comfort at all in the fact
that the words, "Under God," have been added to the Pledge
of Allegiance. And the reference to the Divinity on such
mundane objects as coins and dollar bills outrages our Jewish
sense of the fitness of things. What does the commandment

against taking the Lord's name in vain mean if it does not enjoin us from a casual repetition that belies its awesome meaning? This is mouthing phrases in place of worship—a cheap religiosity in place of religion.

There is a centuries-old tale about a man who came before the Throne of Judgment and complained that although he prayed early and often and his friend prayed only at rare intervals, the latter seemed to be getting preferential treatment. A heavenly voice provided the answer: Even the Lord on high can be bored by meaningless repetition!

So Jews want no part of this religion-by-rote in the public schools. But their most serious objections are raised at the suggestion that "religious values" be made a regular unit of public-school study. The notion of setting aside a special period of the day devoted to moral and spiritual values, as though they were vitamin capsules to be swallowed at prescribed intervals, does violence to the essence of religion as we see it.

Religion can only be truly taught without words, that is, without religious vocabulary. The most spiritually persuasive teacher I have ever had was a Mr. Irwin, who taught me elementary French in the ninth grade. The sweetness of his being, his unassuming manner, the depth of his compassion for humanity, and, above all, his sparkling optimism about the capacities of his students shone through all the declensions and conjugations. He never took time off to teach religion, but there was enough inspiration in the man to move one Jewish youngster in his class to study for the rabbinate— quite an achievement for a Protestant French teacher.

I wish I knew the answers to all the complex problems of religion and the public schools. What about holiday celebrations? Is there a difference between the *observance* of Christmas, which is a sectarian practice, and a *study* of Christmas, which is educational? Is a Christmas play or the singing of hymns merely dramatization, such as the class might undertake in studying the folkways of China, or are they acts of worship? It seems to me that good judgment dictates that, at least in those schools with a considerable Jewish student body, some forbearance be shown on both sides, and an awareness of sensitivities.

The Jewish community is far from alone in these views. Scores of school administrators have voiced their apprehensions about tampering with the historic separation of Church and State. They are justifiably wary of the potentially explosive nature of classroom religious discussion. True, there are those who insist that such discussion is no more controversial than politics. But I don't think we can compare the boiling points of a debate about the relative merits of two political candidates with one concerned with such ultimate questions as what happens to us after we die or whether there really was a virgin birth. Nor would I want the task of selecting and training the teachers who would be assigned to lead such discussions!

It is my frank opinion that the charge of godlessness hurled at today's schools is motivated less by a worry over the schools' neglect of moral training than by chagrin at the schools' successes. A generation ago, when our schools made a far less conscious effort to instill in their youngsters a respect for the sanctity of the individual, a recognition of human equality, and the importance of social co-operation, the churches made little outcry against "secular materialism."

But the very success of the public school in fostering the brotherhood of man without invoking religious sanction has kindled a good deal of resentment. It is a resentment I cannot share. As one committed to a religious interpretation of life, I would prefer that the impulse toward the good life be linked to a belief in God. But my Jewish tradition reminds me that one can come to God through goodness, just as one can come to goodness through God.

# Even Unto the Fourth Generation

ON THE ANZIO BEACHHEAD during World War II, I was attached for a time to a regiment of the 45th Division, taking my meals regularly in a certain company officers' mess. One of the officers with whom I became friendly invariably complained about lack of mail.

"My squaw hardly ever writes," he would say, or: "I haven't heard from my squaw in a month."

Puzzled at such a bizarre expression, I finally asked another officer why this man kept referring to his wife that way. "Jim calls her a squaw because that's what she is. Most of the men in our company are Indians, including me!"

Soon after the end of the war, a shameful incident in Iowa recalled this experience for me. A local cemetery board with a "rule" barring nonwhites, ordered the removal of a body from its grave on learning that the deceased was an American Indian. The fact that he was also a war hero, brought home from an overseas military cemetery, made no difference whatever to these stalwart upholders of their sordid "rule." The body was disinterred lest it "contaminate" the soil for the noble white race. Anthropologists tells us that no primitive tribe on earth would so humiliate the dead!

To me the most frightening aspect of racial bigotry is the total irrationality of this disease. The recent controversy over desegregating the Catholic parochial schools in Louisiana is a case in point. Here was the Church, with all its spiritual and moral authority, reminding its adherents of the Pope's denunciation of racial prejudice as sinful and immoral, and ordering the integration of Church schools. Realistically it must be

89

recognized, of course, that even the devout are capable of sin, even of flagrant violation of the moral law. But it is hard to imagine any other instance in which those who defied the law would dare picket the Bishop's residence to have the law changed, or rush to the press and the TV cameras to denounce their spiritual leaders for attempting to enforce it. The fact that men and women who have been taught to accept the authority of their Church without question suddenly presume to teach the princes of that Church the rights and the wrongs of the faith is a measure of the challenge which the school integration order represents to these people.

An editorial in *Commonweal,* a leading Catholic lay journal, recently pointed out that one reason such a situation could develop is that for so many years the Church—and all the good people in Louisiana, Catholics and otherwise—had accepted the injustices of segregation without protest. There is some measure of validity in the argument that a sin tolerated for almost a century without any effort to erase it could not really be much of a sin in the eyes of religion. Small wonder that a move to change such well-established customs seemed, to some believers, less conviction than caprice.

The racial tensions of the past few years, with their attendant bitterness and frustration for people of all colors, have brought home to me with resounding force a truth I had been avoiding since my middle teens. As a student of the Bible, I always squirmed a little at the words, "I the Lord thy God am a jealous God, visiting the iniquity of the fathers unto the third and the fourth generation of them that hate Me." The first part of this declaration was easily accepted, but I wished somehow that Moses had found a way to tone down the thunder of God's warning that man's sins would not be forgotten.

I understand now that this warning is a basic law of life which none of us can wish out of existence. For what the ancients were telling us, and today's headlines repeat, is that God is a God of justice, and justice is not a caprice of the moment or even of the generation. Justice has no substitute. It has frequently, and at great penalty, been postponed. But it cannot be permanently denied. And the longer it is avoided, the more painful must be the confrontation.

There is a scene in Harper Lee's immensely moving novel *To Kill a Mockingbird* in which a group of genteel Southern ladies discuss with much sadness the plight of some faraway tribe which lacks the advantage of living in a Christian home with Christian folks in a Christian town. Their own community has just been torn apart by the legal "lynching" of an innocent, crippled Negro. The household help has been brooding over the outrage. And with a tremendous conviction of their own piety the ladies urge one another to exercise "Christian charity," and practice "forgiveness" toward their Negro servants: "I tell you, you never ought to let an opportunity go by to witness for the Lord," declares one fine belle.

Too often, too many of us engage in this same spiritual travesty. We prate about "love" and "forgiveness" and ignore that almost basic demand of our God: *Do Justice.*

We Jews have become defensive, even a bit apologetic, about this emphasis on justice in our religion—as though we were extolling a second-class virtue, not in the same league with love. But Judaism tells us, in the commandment which emphasizes God's supremacy over the affairs of man, that if one generation does not remove evil from its midst, the next generation will have to cope with an even greater evil when its time has come. Certainly in the area of American race relations we have seen this evil festering, and we are fast approaching the day of reckoning. In our lifetime we will have to pay the social and moral cost of integrating and digesting a submerged segment of our population. There will be children who must suffer a slower learning pace until other children, kept down by our bigotry, can catch up. There will be communities faced with unsettling changes, as newcomers take their places among the old residents. There will be tension; there may well be violence. And we can no longer postpone these events. For the American Negro has waited, ever since he arrived on these shores in chains, for justice. He is not willing to wait much longer.

Of course there are still millions of Americans hoping that the *next* generation will take care of the problem. There's a little of Louis XIV in all of us, it seems. Let's go about it "gradually," they say. Let's not adopt radical measures, or fly in the face of established mores. And above all, let's not pass laws against discrimination because they don't give people time to "adjust" to the new moral demands.

But if not we, then our children or our children's children will have to come to grips with justice. And I think, for the sake of our children and theirs, *we* had better get on with the job.

Actually, if we really set our minds to it, it may not prove such a forbidding task. Americans so practiced in the art of absorbing millions of poverty-stricken, foreign-tongued immigrants should not be unequal to making 19 million of its own citizens finally feel at home.

If Judaism has anything to teach America in this matter of normal race relations, it would be this: Declare a moratorium on such words as "love" unless you can prove you mean it. The phrase "love thine enemy" has little relevance to life, and is filled with overtones of insufferable condescension that blind us to the true ethical demands of living. We're past the day when it was enough simply to "be kind to our colored friends." What we need now is a hard-headed, realistic affirmation of justice.

I say realistic, because the consequences of rejecting God's law are not yet fully visible. The most eloquent of all the prophets, Amos, cried out: "Three times will I forgive, saith the Lord, but a fourth time I will exact the penalty—for despising the law."

All the world has watched the patience, the tolerant good will, and even the compassion of a Martin Luther King and others like him in the face of outrage after outrage. How long, I ask myself, could I continue to see the children I love turned away from the swings and the seesaws, the schools and the libraries, the parks and the hospitals my taxes helped to pay for? How long would I be willing to look at a map of the United States knowing that most of the thousands of miles of its shore lines are out of bounds for me?

America has thus far escaped disaster primarily because most of the Negro leaders, by the grace of God, have been the Martin Luther Kings and not the angry young men I met in the army. How many Americans know that Negro soldiers guarding Nazi prisoners on a train headed toward Southern prisoner-of-war camps were kept out of the Pullman dining cars while the Germans, who a few weeks before had been busy killing our men, were permitted to eat with the other whites!

"Wait," the Negro GI's told me. "Our day will come!"

We are beginning to realize, intellectually—because the fact is being hammered home to us from every direction—that the white race is a minority in our rapidly shrinking world. But the emotional impact of this fact has yet to reach us. A few years ago I attended a religious conference that brought representatives of over sixty nations to Kobe, Japan. I spent ten exciting days in the company of thoughtful, forward-looking individuals who reflected the world community of which I was but one member. In every meeting room there were three colored delegates for every white one present. It was extremely clear, as one looked around that gathering, that America's traditional posture in race relations could not be maintained.

Ever since the Supreme Court decision of May, 1954, we have been on the threshold of a relatively peaceful revolution. To be sure, there has been violence, and that violence has made headlines. But to me the wonder is that there has been so *little* violence.

There is a tongue-in-cheek Hasidic tale about a disciple of a certain rabbi who boasted of the miracles his master had performed.

"Our rabbi is such a miracle worker," he explained, "that once when he came to a town full of skeptics, who mocked and heckled him while he was preaching a sermon, he ordered the four walls of the synagogue to collapse, to punish the sinners for their disbelief. And when some of his disciples pleaded: 'Rabbi, have mercy! Innocent women and children will die with the mockers!' the kind-hearted rabbi invoked a *second* miracle, even greater than the first, and ordered the four walls of the synagogue to stand in their place."

I can only hope that the walls of America remain intact while we address ourselves to the prodigious task of restoring dignity to ourselves and our fellow citizens. Perhaps there is yet time.

# *Belonging, Believing, and Behaving*

# Belonging, Believing, and Behaving

THE PHRASE "religious revival" is widely in the news, among Jews just as it is among Christian Americans. But although everyone talks about it, not everyone seems to be really convinced. Again and again, people ask me, "Are we Jews truly in the midst of a religious revival?"

Professor Mordecai Kaplan has answered this question in a most provocative way, and in typical Jewish fashion, by posing another question: What level are you talking about, he asks—the level of belonging, believing, or experiencing?

Certainly, on the level of belonging, be it formal affiliation or informal identification, Judaism has achieved a degree of visibility unmatched in modern history. Since the end of World War II, there's been no business like *shul* business. In 1947, I addressed a congregation in Roslyn, Long Island, in a rented upstairs room in a fraternal club house. Today that group includes two flourishing temples of close to one thousand families each. So, too, in Levittown. Religious-school figures in the suburbs are 20 to 70 per cent higher than they were in the big urban areas a few years back.

Dr. Albert Gordon's books on Jews in suburbia report a similar growth all over the country. Nineteen new congregations were organized in the San Fernando Valley in two years' time—and this is not simply a reflection of mobility. These new congregations had not been affiliated with a synagogue in their home towns of Chicago or New York.

Yet, many who study this trend caution that we have little reason for self-congratulation.

97

Professor Nathan Glazer, in his University of Chicago study, *American Judaism*, points out that we must distinguish between Judaism and Jewishness. In Jewishness, clearly, we have prospered. In Judaism, in a sense of faith, piety, religious conviction, we have not.

Similarly, in a study of Jewish students at Harvard University, the key word is identification. Jewish young men in America today, this report indicates, have a strong sense of Jewish identification, a group attachment, but not a religious experience.

Let's not carry this note of pessimism too far, however. I see precious value, even on this primal level, in the mere feeling of belonging.

I wish it were possible to transmit a feeling of belonging by teaching—by some kind of intellectual communication. But you can't. It's the warm tug at the heart that comes when, in some distant land, you meet someone from your own town: the quickening of spirit when you discover that the stranger is also wearing a fraternity pin or a Hadassah insignia, or that he also went to old P. S. 96.

Aristotle observed, many centuries ago, that not to belong is to die. Man is a social animal. Outside a group, life is meaningless.

There's a word for this feeling of belonging, a word our old folks loved—*Yiddishkeit*. By *Yiddishkeit* I mean that comfortable at-homeness in the company we share together; the family feeling which hovers over a people whose forefathers have been through so much together, in joy and sorrow, bright climes and gray; above all, that abiding sense of destiny; that gratifying consciousness of common historic purpose.

Thus, my heart gladdens when all the studies indicate a growing sense of "belonging" on the part of American Jews, even if the depth of their identification does not seem very great. But, as Dr. Kaplan observes, our lives must really be lived in more than one dimension—on more than one level. And if there are some who need only the cement of belonging for their self-fulfillment, there are others, I am happy to say, for whom Jewish experience would be vapid were they so restricted. The Chinese philosopher-writer, Dr. Lin Yutang, once autographed a book for me with his favorite Confucian saying, "A little too much is just enough for me." My own philosophy is this: "A little bit more is just enough for me." That little bit more is a faith, a believing, an overpowering presence in my life, a conviction that embraces my soul and is as necessary to me as the very air I breathe.

Does modern man believe? Do any of us believe, as Maimonides put it, *be-emunah shlemah,* "with complete and unflagging conviction"? Only the other day, in my study, someone told me, "Oh, we are not very religious in our family; we're Reform Jews from way back." As though to believe with intelligence were not genuine belief; as though one could not feel deeply or be moved profoundly by a faith that commends itself to the modern mind.

*Lo vashamayim*—"These ideals are not in the heavens, but at our very feet." Life has purpose and meaning. We believe that one human being can transform his world, his generation, his community. We have confidence that there will come a time, not just in the prayer book but in the experience of man, when we will fashion a society founded on intelligence and good will; when the absurdities of race prejudice will be relics of a benighted past, and the shadows of atomic terror but a dim nightmare out of man's childhood. We believe it, not only because the Prophet says so, not only because we articulate the words in the Adoration, but because we know that man is fashioned in the image of God.

To my mind, the tragedy of contemporary Judaism is the fact that the synagogue has lost some of the most sensitive and dedicated Jews of our generation. It grieves me when such consecrated servants of mankind as Dr. Jonas Salk, or the Nobel Prize winner, biologist Joshua Lederberg, tell reporters: "Oh, we don't work at our religion."

Why is it that Dr. Selman Waksman does not view his lifesaving discoveries in antibiotics and his generous renunciation of all financial gain from these efforts as the highest expression of his Jewish faith?

How is it that editor Norman Cousins, who has devoted so much of his energies to helping the Japanese girls disfigured at Hiroshima and the Polish victims of Nazi medical experimentations, and who has worked so hard in the campaign to abolish the dangerous, air-poisoning nuclear tests—how is it that Mr. Cousins fails to acknowledge, even to himself, that his Jewish heritage is in back of such shining idealism?

Many of my colleagues censure Jewish intellectuals, scientists, and writers for their disloyalty to Judaism. But I'm afraid my fellow rabbis miss the mark. Many in the literary and scientific community, born of Jewish parentage, are lost to organized Judaism for a number of cogent reasons.

In the first place, their image of the Jewish faith is generally as childlike as their understanding of science is mature. They reject the six-year-old's notion of a God who is little more than a policeman, because they have never been exposed to a more mature version of their faith. They may have read hundreds of books by Huxley and even Tillich, and Niebuhr —but do they know the writings of Martin Buber, Milton Steinberg, or Mordecai Kaplan?

In the second place, the synagogue has failed wretchedly in articulating the creed of the modern Jew, and the tremendous moral demands and sacrifices which Judaism makes on modern man.

And certainly many sensitive, intellectual young Jews have been repelled by the frequent vulgarization of American synagogue life—the New York synagogues listed in the "Yellow Pages" under "Catering"; the Bar Mitzvah affairs that are not celebrations but extravaganzas; the garment district synagogues where, on the last day of a festival, you can say a quick *Kaddish* for a quarter.

Judaism has so much to say to our finest minds, to our most idealistic young people. But we need the wisdom and farsightedness to find the path to their hearts. Only then can we expect them to participate in the deeper level of Judaism, the level of belief.

Finally, to be a Jew means not only belonging and believing. It involves what Mordecai Kaplan calls "experiencing"—and what I like to call "behaving." Behaving in a pattern of life which represents the climax of belonging and belief. *Lo Hadmidrash ikor eloh ha-maaseh*—"Doing is the key to faith," the ancient rabbis taught.

To belong and to believe is to enrich *oneself*. To translate our beliefs into concrete action for others is the ultimate goal of faith.

What, then, does the particular system of belief known as Judaism have to commend itself to modern man? First, it is the product of thousands of years of continuous thought by thoughtful people. A Chinese philosopher once explained to me why Judaism and Confucianism have so many parallels: "You see, Rabbi," he said, "we are both an old people—we, five thousand years old, you, four thousand. When you live long enough, you gain insights into the human heart and human relations!"

Second, while creating and maintaining the institutions necessary for the transmission of its beliefs, Judaism has had the maturity and wisdom to avoid making its clergy and its synagogue the objects of worship.

But Judaism's major strength and sophistication lies in its understanding that symbols, though necessary to religion, are only the *means* to an end, not the ends in themselves. They are the flowers one sends to a beloved, not the love one bears; the ring on the bride's finger, not the enduring devotion that is the real quality of marriage. Symbols are the language in which a faith describes itself and makes itself heard.

The symbolism of Yom Kippur, for example, can best be understood in these terms. Why do we fast on this day? For four basic reasons, decrees our tradition.

We fast to demonstrate our remorse for our sins of the past year. We fast as a form of self-discipline, to prove to ourselves that as we can control our appetite, so can we also manage other trivial, vain, and self-seeking impulses within us. We fast to divert our attention from the physical to the spiritual, to dramatize the fact that man is much more than the beast of the field. The pious Jew will channel the hours he saves by not eating to prayer, to meditation, to candid self-appraisal.

But, finally, say the rabbis, we fast to evoke compassion within us. We know, because we have read the statistics, that two out of three people in the world go to bed hungry every night. But these facts do not really register with us, any more than the word "color" registers with a blind man. The average person in *our* world never experiences hunger and thirst, except as a matter of choice. We impose upon ourselves the pangs of an empty stomach once a year to help feel more keenly the real needs of others.

Judaism, with the wisdom of the centuries, bids us pray and fast, so that by chastening and purifying our spirits we can live more tenderly, more compassionately, more creatively, with our fellow man.

# Be It Ever So Hectic

THE OTHER DAY, in our suburban community, I was discussing the problem of parental discipline with the mother of three children.

"Oh, I have no trouble showing my authority. My children know I mean business when they deserve punishment," she explained in all earnestness. "When I tell them they can only watch TV *in black and white,* I really mean it."

I can well imagine the blanket of gloom which envelops that household when the color TV is darkened until the children have atoned for their sins.

Our Westchester town is like dozens of gilded ghettos in the suburbs—Highland Park, Illinois; Cleveland Heights, Ohio; Elkins Park, Pennsylvania. . . . Not long ago, when I was taking a turn as local car-pool driver, I eavesdropped a bit on the conversation of my youthful charges:

"Jonathan," a nine-year-old neighbor asked my young son, "how often have you been to Europe?"

Looking down at his shoes, Jonny mumbled that he had been abroad once.

"Eleven years old, and you've only been to Europe *once?*" She sighed pityingly. Her latest trip had been her fifth.

Our neighborhood teen-agers, comparing notes after a vacation period, make casual mention of Bermuda, the Virgin Islands, Hawaii, Jamaica, and all points north, east, south, or west. They are quick to commiserate with the poor girl who cries: "I'm sick and tired of going to Florida, year after year."

One reads a great deal these days about the overprivileged, emotionally impoverished youngsters of our affluent society

whose parents give much of their means but little of themselves. Certainly this is one facet of life today that is frequently
observed. But I have a feeling the problem is even more
complicated.

I am not convinced, for example, that the third-generation
child sees less of his father and mother than did children of
the immigrant generation, whose parents were busy grappling
for an economic foothold. Why, then, is the image of the old-
fashioned family so warm for these children now grown? Is it
all the product of embroidered fantasy—a glow of memory
quite unrelated to reality? Isn't it true that today's parents,
by and large, spend more hours with their children than their
parents ever did?

I never went bowling with my father. On one occasion he
did take his children to a hockey game, but he made the
mistake of sitting behind the net, where a flying puck caught
him above the eye. After a few stitches were taken, he decided that New World games were for gentiles only, and we
never saw him at a sports event again. Nevertheless, my
brothers and sisters and I felt no sense of deprivation. The
child's world—and later the youth's world—was not within the
adult domain and we were perfectly content with the peaceful
coexistence of this arrangement.

In my youth, we never conceived of "togetherness" as joint
parent-child amusement or entertainment. We thought it perfectly obvious that the excitements and enjoyments of childhood could not possibly be shared by adults, unless they were
emotionally retarded. By the same token, young people who
found satisfaction in adult pleasures were considered old
before their time.

But there were countless ways in which we enjoyed real
"togetherness." One of the most vivid memories of my childhood revolves around our giving up bed and bedroom to new
cousins who had just emigrated to Canada. Their first home
was our home, and while the major financial sacrifice was
borne by my parents, all of us were called on to deny ourselves something—a bit of privacy, a planned vacation, a

longed-for bicycle, all were postponed for a year. And in this enterprise, the convenience, the plans, the self-denials, the pleasures, and the frustrations of all the family were fused together. What emerged was a precious family purpose, very different from the superficial union that so often passes for "togetherness" today.

The reason "togetherness" has fallen from grace in our eyes is that we've discovered this superficiality. Playing together is a bland substitute for *feeling* together, and *experiencing life* together, whether in joy or in sorrow.

Our contemporary values are reflected in the negative connotation we give to such words as "clannishness" and "tribalism." To cling to one's own clan is deemed undesirable; to be bound up too closely with one's tribe is considered a primitive trait.

Jewish tradition, though, has always praised and prized tight family cohesion. The *mishpochah,* or family clan, was a powerful force for righteousness in the community. A family member hesitated long before breaking the moral code, for he knew that his misdeeds cast a long shadow over every one of his kin.

Somehow this concern with family identity and responsibility did not negate or lessen the Jewish passion for individuality. For uniqueness, in Jewish tradition, was a gift from God: each human being was a special child of God, requiring no intermediary, no advocate. He stood before the bar of divine judgment alone. In the eyes of society, however, an individual was judged largely in the context of *family*. He shared all of the responsibilities of the family and was comforted by the knowledge that all the members of his clan stood behind him, sharing in his concerns and his destiny.

The modern home, everyone tells us, is child-centered, rather than adult-centered. In Judaism this is an invalid distinction. The home ought to be *family*-centered, not a tug of war between the generations.

How can we put our finger on the nature of today's family discontent? Is the modern parent's plaint any different from the ancient Athenian's anguish about "the younger generation"? And are today's youthful rebellions any different from those of their parents before them?

I think there *is* a difference. I am convinced that the problems of our age are without precedent, both in the degree of acrimony and the width of the chasm separating the generations.

When I ask the mother of a teen-ager how her youngster is doing, the muscles of her face tighten, a cloud passes over her eyes, and her lips quiver: "Do parents ever survive. . . ?" Many a parent of a young lady about to march down the aisle, whispers to me: "We just made it! Now let him do the worrying."

The crisis mood is not confined to one social or economic class or to one country. In Tel Aviv, in London, in Rome, I hear similar cries of parental woe. Some of the frustration is caused by our vague family relationships. In the traditional family, each member had a clearly defined role. The parent was provider, protector, and mentor. The child was expected to receive loving care, to respond with respect and affection, and to share in the fortunes and misfortunes of the family. It was the parent's responsibility to teach—and the child's to learn.

That uncomplicated arrangement is a thing of the past. My grandfather had access to 90 per cent of his child's mind and heart; my father could reach 50 per cent of mine; but my influences upon my child are in constant competition with a great many others invading his consciousness—radio, television, newspapers, his peer group, his teachers, those vague influences making up the mores of our contemporary culture. Certainly I want to pass my values down. The most important injunction in Judaism is: "Thou shalt teach them diligently unto thy children." But the modern parent must first determine what he will be diligent about. Our children cannot be expected to live carbon copies of our lives in their world. It's a very different world from the one we grew up in. When to accept this difference and when to resist it—that is our dilemma.

A further strain on parent-child relations is the lack of opportunity for personal fulfillment. Our tradition has much to say about the joys and satisfactions of our own toil. The do-it-yourself cult is not a modern development. The Talmud describes two rabbis of the second century, Judah and Simeon, who came to the academy, one bearing a jug he had made with his own hands, the other a basket he had woven. "Great is handicraft, for it honors those who engage in it," they explained.

Our young people, especially those who grow up in typical middle-class communities, rarely move beyond the "arts and crafts" stage of do-it-yourself in any area of their lives. Our social incubation period now covers a third or more of man's life span, and children remain dependent even into the early years of marriage. Sports and entertainment are not the only aspects of living relegated to the spectator's arena. Politics, economics, social stability, questions of war and peace, all seem to require nothing more of us than grandstand viewing.

Small wonder, then, that child-parent relations are so often acrimonious. For what the young are really demanding to know is why their elders have failed to provide a securer world, while their parents, helpless to provide this one necessity, grumble about the ingratitude of a generation which "has everything."

Logic would dictate that a carefree young generation, liberated from most of the insecurities which marked every previous one, would be relaxed and calm. Our children ought to regard themselves as the most privileged youth in human history, for every gift of science, art, and literature, every economic and social opportunity has been placed at their feet.

Are we faced then with churlish ingratitude—a generation whose moral fiber has been corroded by indulgence? I don't think so. The profound resentment of our youth—and it is profound, though not necessarily conscious—is against the larger world which we have provided, along with these superficial delicacies. For more essential than comfort is a sense

of certainty—among other things a certainty that there will
be a tomorrow. The youth of the Atomic Age no longer have
that assurance. We have not even provided them with a certainty about themselves, about their roles as individuals in a
complex impersonal corporate society—a certainty that they
count in the universe.

We can't turn back to a warmer, less threatening era, much
as we would like to do so. But we *can* face up to the dangers
that threaten us and do what we can, together, to cope with
them. Children who grow up knowing they are expected to
*give* as well as take, to do their share in the family, the classroom, the community, and the world—these children feel
needed and useful, not helpless and angry. And parents who
give of *themselves* to their family, their group, their community, and their country, these parents also feel useful and
needed instead of guilty and angry.

I think that somehow the anger between the generations
would fade a good deal if parents *and* children could feel
they were really engaged in the do-it-yourself task of ordering their world as much as they can, together.

# Motives of Men

THE SPIRIT OF Rosh Hashanah is compounded of two themes—or more accurately, a theme and a countertheme. The New Year is certainly an occasion of joy. Our homes, our temple, everything around us reverberates with the sound of good wishes.

Yet, the countertheme of this day is equally insistent. It is a solemn day . . . *Yom Hadin,* "the Day of Judgment," a Day of Fear and Trembling. The traditional liturgy declares that on this day humans are like sheep passing before the Supreme Shepherd, one by one. On this day, God sits in judgment upon us, knowing and seeing our innermost thoughts, both good and evil.

How oppressive this Day of Reckoning would have been for our pious grandparents, were it not for their faith that the God who knew all was an *El Rachum Vechanun,* "a compassionate and forgiving God," who understands that we are frail mortals and is ready to give us another chance if there is genuine repentance in our hearts.

This is a repeated emphasis in Judaism: God as the Judge who penetrates the recesses of our hearts. And along with this, the constant reminder that God, *not man,* is the Judge.

One of the most depressing aspects of the cynicism which marks so many of our relationships these days is the casual, thoughtless way we undertake to play God—to judge the motives of men. We used to speak bitterly of our age as the era of "what's in it for me?" Actually there is much more destructiveness in the chorus, "What's in it for him?"

A political leader presents a brilliant address or writes a

scintillating book, and we arch an eyebrow; What young Ph.D. ghost wrote that? The president of a corporation heads a charitable campaign, and we assume that this is a deal cooked up at the Twenty-One Club by the public relations counsel of the firm and the public relations director of the charity.

We are all so supersophisticated, so adept at looking under the surface, so alert to the dangers of hidden persuaders and mass manipulators, that every action of our neighbor is suspect.

Thus, when Governor Nelson Rockefeller of New York issued a scathing denunciation of the Administration's foreign policy a few months back, not a single commentator, not a single editorial writer, ventured the thought that Mr. Rockefeller may have said what he did because he honestly believed it. Is it possible, just barely possible, that as a father, a grandfather, a thinking citizen, the Governor is really worried about where our country is going? What a strange, improbable idea!

What's in it for him? What "team" developed this "line"? Is his eye on 1964 or 1968?

In our own circles, too, we are constantly confronted with this cynicism. A friend or an acquaintance takes on the chairmanship of a charity campaign, joins the board of a church or congregation, or offers to head a PTA affair. Why did he do it? Why did she accept? Immediately we become assistants to the Almighty. We peer into the hearts of others, and we say, without a moment's hesitation, "Some people can't live without honors." Or, "It's good for his business." Or, "She wants to sit up front where everyone will see her Paris creation."

Often these jaundiced views of human behavior are set forth in the impressive language of dynamic psychology. The United States has some fifty thousand trained analysts and a hundred million self-proclaimed ones. Equipped with such verbal ammunition as "ego satisfaction," "compensation," "sublimation," and so on, we can sit back smugly while a bazaar chairman works his fingers to the bone, nod our head clinically, as we imagine Dr. Freud might have done, and declare sagely: "Of course, *we* know what makes Sammy run for office!"

A bit of joy is drained from life each time we witness an act of self-sacrifice and mar it with the unpleasant query, "What's *really* behind it?" Have we gained anything at all when we read an inspiring biography—of Theodor Herzl, for example—only to ask ourselves "What *really* made him do it?" Are we something the wiser because we come home from seeing *The Miracle Worker* with the nagging suspicion that Anne Sullivan was engaged in ego-striving when she brightened Helen Keller's darkness? There's much vicarious *nachas* in the contemplation of somebody joyfully and unselfishly engaged in acts of goodness.

Our ruthless dissection of men's motives has discouraged some of our ablest, most gifted people from public service. Part of the crisis in leadership, on every level, can be laid at the doorstep of those little souls who embarrass men of stature with petty doubts about their sincerity.

Let us not forget that each time we judge others in this fashion we are also judging ourselves. For even if we are prepared to believe, with utter arrogance, that we alone are capable of performing out of purity of heart, we must face the fact that others will apply this same cynicism to our own actions. Every time we indulge in this querulous searching after "What's in it for him?" we draw a tinier image of ourselves.

In international affairs we also frequently exhibit what our prayer book calls the sin of false judgment. We assume that each nation acts, by definition, solely out of national self-interest. Professor Reinhold Niebuhr, in his many writings, beginning with *Moral Man and Immoral Society*, declares that we justify, on the highest moral and religious grounds, acts of government that have one clear motivation, the security and the welfare of the State.

But there are times when even a country can and does engage in acts of pure, unselfish goodness, the noblest of virtues. Some time ago, when Chile was devastated by an earthquake, our Government's hands went out in sympathetic friendship —simply because there was suffering, and we as a nation could help.

Yet the inevitable negative spirit of our times sees every American action grounded in national aggrandizement. Did we dispatch doctors to the Congo in order to head off epidemic? Yes, but we were there to compete with Soviet teams. Did we ship wheat and corn to India and Ceylon? Of course, but only to create a favorable image of America among the uncommitted peoples. We have more than one motive for our actions—and therefore, the cynics insist, all of our motives are evil.

Our Jewish sages, mature and realistic, long ago appreciated the fact that every man's motives are mixed. Just think of our own minds and hearts. Is it not true that often, in our most sacrificial moments, there is the vagrant feeling of personal pleasure in the essentially selfless deed? As parents, we frequently deny ourselves for the sake of our children—and also for the keen delight we feel in the growth and development these denials make possible.

In the past four years the State of Israel has dispatched hundreds of technicians, medical experts, agronomists, civic administrators—men whom it sorely needs—to Ghana, to Burma, to Nigeria, and to other Afro-Asian countries. Why this relief program on the part of a country itself so hard pressed? There are two operating motives. One, a political motive, is dictated by the fact that a besieged country needs allies to maneuver itself out of Nasser's stranglehold. But the fundamental driving force is an ethical one, drawn out of the Biblical injunction: "Ye shall be a light unto the nations"; drawn from the Talmudic teaching: "Even the poorest among you shall give to charity"; drawn from the wisdom of Maimonides, who taught that the greatest *mitzvah* of *Tzdakah* lies in helping a man to help himself.

Prime Minister Ben-Gurion, a profound student of Jewish tradition, never tires of pointing out that Israel did not come into being again merely to add another flag to the United

Nations. Israel is not a Madagascar, a Cyprus, a Viet-Nam, a geographic entity born out of accidental circumstances. Israel has a covenant with God, a rendezvous with divine history. Once it was a land and a people which gave the world a moral force that still spells the difference between barbarism and civilization. It is this kind of land, this kind of people, that Israel strives to be once again.

Yes, Israel's motives in helping her neighbors are mixed as are so many motives of so many nations, groups, and people. *But the dominant ingredient is the one that counts.*

"There are those who come into a situation for ulterior motives," said our rabbis, "but remain for pure reasons."

# Our Minor Sins

EACH YEAR, on Yom Kippur eve, the strange and mysterious magnet of *Kol Nidre* draws Jews warmly into its embrace, and all the children of Israel everywhere stand in silent awe of that which is holy in life.

What compelling force gathers us together in one mighty congregation?

Is it fear—undefined, disquieting fear? Perhaps the ancients were right, and Yom Kippur is truly the Day of Judgment, when the Supreme Judge examines each of us, saint and sinner alike, and marks our cards "pass" or "fail."

Is it reminiscence that beckons us—family memories of small, crowded, airless synagogues, where fathers wrapped themselves in prayer shawls, and mothers dropped their tears on old and worn prayer books, while they pleaded with a merciful God to be good to us, their children? For many of us, *Kol Nidre* night is a lump-in-the-throat occasion.

As some people do not know, we Jews have our confessional, a confessional just as meaningful and spiritually moving as that of our Roman Catholic friends. In some ways, the Jewish rite of confession is similar to the Catholic. Jewish tradition dictates that on Yom Kippur a man recite the formal catalogue of sins in public, and—to quote an old source— "when he knows that he has committed one particular sin, he ought to cry as he mentions it, and confess with particular emotion." If there is an unlisted sin of which he is guilty, he ought to confess it from the depths of his heart. "If his sin is well known, he ought to confess it loudly."

That custom is not too different from that of the ancient and medieval Church. As the historian George Foot Moore describes it: "Restoration [for the sinner] was possible only by way of public penitence solemnly undertaken in the presence of the church, and proceeded only by slow stages."

Both Jew and Catholic are required to express their penitence before their fellow man, but there is a crucial difference. Since the year 1215, when the Church made it an obligation for all the faithful, Catholicism has held that a man's sin is against the *Church itself,* and can only be forgiven by an official of the Church. But the object of the Jewish confessional is never to convey information about one person's weakness to another. For the Jew, sin is a private and personal matter, a relationship between one man and one God. In Catholicism, the Church is the representative of God on earth. *The Synagogue, whether traditional or liberal, is God's home, not His office.* All spiritual contact runs directly from man's heart to God's presence.

I have always been impressed by the fact that the transgressions we list in these Yom Kippur prayers do not include the major sins. We do not beat our breasts and declare: "Forgive our sins of killing, of stealing, of adultery." We speak only of disrespect, of stubbornness, of evil meditations. Why? Is our prayer book too squeamish, too gentle, too circumspect? I don't think so.

The transgressions of which most of us are guilty are not the cardinal ones, the once-in-a-lifetime, twice-in-a-lifetime sins. What corrodes our spirit, what nibbles away at our souls, are our tiny, almost imperceptible faults. It is these little sins that are most destructive, for we live and work and play in a society which sanctions—indeed encourages—*petty* larcenies, *petty* cheating, *minor* breaches of good taste.

An ancient Talmudic law declares that when you pass your neighbor's house you may not pick a single splinter off his fence on the theory that he will not miss it. For if all his neighbors did the same, there would soon be no fence. How often do we, in casual conversation, scratch a trifle off our neighbor's reputation in a passing snide remark, a seemingly innocuous comment. And how strangely inconsistent we are. Any gossip in which *we* indulge is, we are convinced, minor, casual, merely a passing of the time of day. But when we become the *objects* of these same comments, those who speak of us are vicious, malicious creatures who use their tongues to detroy a fellow human being.

Our society looks askance at anyone who insists that principle is principle; that truth cannot be bent; that honesty has no exceptions. In our culture, such a person is regarded as overfastidious, probably a candidate for the psychiatrist's couch. In high school it's the sissy who won't allow his neighbor to glance at his examination paper. In business the approximate truth is often all we demand of ourselves. Yet the fact is that a society built on 95 per cent truth, on 95 per cent integrity, inexorably destroys itself.

We are all quite clear on this fact when it comes to the world of sports. Among those who take their golf seriously, how long would a player last who moved the ball surreptitiously, who stopped counting after he reached 6? And woe betide the bridge player who earns the reputation of calling signals. Without scrupulous honesty and unimpeachable fairness, it just isn't worth holding the cards in your hands. Our harsh standards are based on an elementary principle . . . cheating destroys the very fabric of the game so that it no longer makes any sense.

Yet in the greatest game of all, the game of life, how often we rationalize about our departures from truth, from integrity, from fairness!

Last year, as a tourist in Italy, I walked through the magnificent ruins of ancient Pompeii. On the main street is a drinking fountain that stood in the middle of the thoroughfare for centuries before the Common Era. The guide pointed out where the water had gushed forth and, amazingly, the spot on the marble where people placed the four fingers of their hand to lean over for a drink. There, etched in the marble are the deep indentations of a human palm and four fingers. Incredible? It is hard to imagine that a hand leaning on a piece of marble would leave a mark. But do it for four hundred years and the hand might as well be a chisel.

Our souls are very much like that marble: A little bit of cheating, a tiny grain of gossip, the mere suggestion of larceny, may seem to leave no imprint. But the accumulation is a corrosion of conscience, an eating away of character, so that each time another Yom Kippur comes around, and we catalogue our minor frailties, we are lesser persons than we were the year before.

# What Kind of Atonement?

IN JULY, 1961, I sat in a courtroom in Jerusalem, watching Adolf Eichmann on the witness stand.

How can I describe the feeling churning inside of me as I looked at one of Hitler's chief executioners? So many millions of words have already been written on the subject that there is little new anyone can add. In a recent interview, I tried to convey a little of the atmosphere of the trial. It was more like a graduate seminar at a university than a courtroom. The hall itself was an auditorium, used only temporarily for these judicial proceedings. Everyone was so painfully polite, it was hard to sense any feeling of an accuser and an accused.

On this particular day, Judge Halevy spent several hours cross-examining Eichmann. The tone of his voice was not one bit harsh or unkind. He seemed to be saying: "As a guest expert, Mr. Eichmann, who knows so much more about the subject than we do, what do you think about Holland as compared to Hungary?" There was an academic quality about it all, as though I were back in college, and the professor had invited a learned colleague to share his knowledge with the class.

And Adolf Eichmann was unmoved and unhurried. He consulted his notes, spoke deliberately. Obviously he was not as eager as the rest of the world for the trial to end.

(One parenthetical observation: As the reports of the trial indicated, all of Eichmann's guards were Oriental Jews; the Israelis did not risk using men who might have been related to his victims. So all the jailers and courtroom police were Jews from Asia and Africa. But what astonished me was the

118

absence of such Jews in the audience. I saw not one Oriental Jew among the hundreds of men and women watching the proceedings. Why? Were they not permitted to attend or, as is more likely, didn't they apply for admission? And if Jews who were not directly affected by Hitler's onslaught have little interest in the Eichmann trial, how deep is the concern of my fellow Americans who are not of the Jewish faith?)

On the particular day that I was present, Eichmann made his historic plea for special consideration: "Let me be an atonement for the German people," he said. "Let me live and teach German youth the mistakes of the past."

The words fascinated me: "Let me be an atonement." I wondered what kind of atonement Eichmann had in mind when he used that word.

Certainly not a Jewish atonement . . . a *kapporah.* Not even a Christian atonement. Our grandparents had two customs relating to the High Holy Days. Some of them used to *shlag kapporos.* They would buy a chicken, symbolically place their sins upon it, and wave it over their heads, as though to drive away sin. *Shlaggen* means to smite, to strike an object in atonement. It was also the custom, among the more pious, to bring a strap to the synagogue on the eve of Yom Kippur and ask the sexton to deliver a few well-placed strokes on the back, as atonement for the year's sins.

Primitive as these customs seem, there is a genuine moral quality in them. For atonement, to be real, must involve a certain amount of self-flagellation. Certainly for modern man it cannot be a physical act of self-punishment. But psychologically, repentance, or *tshuvah,* must entail some measure of agonizing regret.

To me the tragedy of the Eichmann trial, and the moral import of it, lies in the ethical posture of the defendant. On the day after we arrived, Judge Halevy sermonized: "Herr Eichmann, all that you have heard has had no more effect on you than a drop of water on a hot rock. Why don't you show courage and admit responsibility for the things that happened? You yourself admitted during the course of the trial that the

German people lacked civic courage. Now, if you examine your conscience, you would admit that you lacked civic courage!"

And Eichmann answered, "Yes, like many others."

I have sinned, declared the Nazi, *but so did many others.*

I asked myself as I made my way from the air-conditioned courtroom to the heat of the Jerusalem day, What kind of atonement is the world now ready to make?

The German people today, led by the Adenauers and the Willi Brandts . . . do they understand the true nature of atonement? It means much more than indemnification. German restitution was a fine gesture. It had in it some element of regret, as though the family of a murderer had offered compensation to the family of his victim. But the major moral question remains: Can it happen again? Have the German people made atonement by becoming different from what they were, more democratic in their educational life, their family life, their entire life-style? Do they consider democracy and regard for the rights of Jews merely good public relations, or good in and of itself?

How many people in Germany today feel with Adolf Eichmann that what they did was wrong, but that they simply couldn't help themselves? Versailles drove them to it; the economic crash forced them into it; outside influences were responsible for it all. Unless the German people can confront their own souls and *shlag kapporos*—not just beat their breasts outwardly for the world to behold, but beat themselves inwardly, where it really hurts—then what happened before will inevitably happen again.

Let me confess that when the Free World musters its defenses on behalf of West Berlin, I cannot help but agonize over what kind of Berlin we are willing to make supreme sacrifices for . . . willing to invite atomic missiles on our doorsteps for. Have the people we are now promising to protect truly sought atonement for the sins of the past?

George Bernard Shaw once said: "The wisest man I ever met is my tailor. Each year, when I order a new suit, he measures me all over again. This wise man of a tailor realizes that the George Bernard Shaw of last year is not the same George Bernard Shaw of this year."

That is the true test of the spirit of *tshuvah,* of repentance, of atonement. Are we the same persons we were last year? If so, we enter ill prepared for the Day of Atonement. Yom Kippur is not a time for beating our neighbor's breast, for declaring *thou* hast sinned—even if *thou* in this instance is a creature named Eichmann.

An editorial writer in the *New York Times,* at the close of the trial, caught the spirit of what I mean in more eloquent words than I could ever pen. He said: "Is there anything the judges of Israel can do to impress upon humanity the enormity of the crime of which Eichmann was an accomplice and is now a symbol? Perhaps the most appropriate fate for Eichmann would be to keep him imprisoned for the rest of his natural life, looking out on the new country full of hope and promise that he did so much . . . and so unwillingly . . . to create.

"What was the object and the justification of the trial? It was and it is to do all that can be done to eradicate an evil thing out of our civilization . . . a thing so incredibly wicked that it would not have been believable of modern man if it had not actually occurred. This evil, this wickedness began with intolerance and hate in a few men's hearts. It spread until it almost wrecked the world. Now the obligation is to remember, not in hate, not in the spirit of revenge, but so that this spirit cannot ever flourish again so long as man remains on earth. And to this end, let us begin, each of us, by looking into our own hearts."

# Thou Shalt Choose Life

IT IS HARD TO FIND many passages more poignant than the final words of Moses to the Israelites as they approach the Land of Promise. As he prepares for death on Nebo's lonely mountainside, Moses wonders what will happen to these people after he is gone.

"I call heaven and earth to witness against you this day," he warns them. "I have set before you life and death, the blessing and the curse; *therefore choose life.*"

At first, this seems an almost absurd choice. After all, it would hardly seem necessary to tell anyone that, given the choice of life or death, he ought to choose life. What deeper passion marks our existence than the will to live? Schopenhauer once said that if a man were placed on a bare island, in the middle of a bleak ocean, where there was forever night, forever storm, forever silence, he would still want to live on and on.

Yet when Moses enjoined his followers, ". . . choose life," he was enunciating one of the most profound and unique thoughts in the entire history of mankind's search for religious truth. For it was precisely this choice *for* life which marked the Semitic tribe known as Hebrews and set them apart from all the other tribes around them.

Almost all the primitive peoples were animists. But the ancient animists made little distinction between that which was endowed with a life impulse, and that which was not. A vast variety of ritual acts were designed to imbue a stone, a pillar of wood, a shadow in the night, with symbolic life. But not so the Jews!

To me, one of the most baffling mysteries of Jewish religious history is the almost hysterical rejection of idol worship by the ancient Hebrews. As we mature in our understanding, we sometimes ask: Why were these patriarchs, prophets, and priests so disturbed, so panicky, about idol worship? After all, it seems clear that even the primitives knew in their heart of hearts that the stone figures they paid obeisance to were only symbols of something live and real!

Yet our ancestors carved deeply into our tradition the words of this commandment: "Thou shalt not make any graven image." It was *life* that counted—*people*, not things. *Life* was to be cherished; *life* was to be prized; and man could not breathe life into that which had none.

Abraham, and later Moses, and still later Jeremiah, perceived the great miracle of life three thousand years before Dr. Alexis Carrel and other modern scientists. The ancient Jews said to themselves: All the human wisdom in the world cannot create a single growing fingernail, let alone a human heart which pumps blood at the rate of fourteen thousand quarts an hour.

What is the Jewish reaction in the face of this marvelous work of God's creation?

Above all else, Judaism constantly dwells on *tzar baale chayim,* a tender compassion for all living things. Does the hunter have the right to point a weapon of destruction at an innocent deer, whose simplest part of the body all human skill combined cannot duplicate?

Nor is it an accident that Jews have historically shown such an interest in, and a proclivity for, the practice of medicine. The ancient Ben Sira, of the second century B.C.E., justified tampering with God's work by insisting that a human being is a partner of the divine. So too Maimonides, centuries later. I have never understood those religious doctrines which insist that we cannot interfere with the processes of nature. Of course we should, when such interference adds to life and the living. The orthodontist does, and the optometrist. Certainly the modern surgeon is often a "partner with God"! "Choose

you life" . . . and for the physician faced with the tragic
dilemma of mother or unborn infant, Judaism has a simple,
uncomplicated answer. The mother who is alive and upon
whom responsibilities already rest must be preserved.

Is there a Jewish way of looking at life? Yes, there *is* something that is distinctively Jewish, though this should not be
interpreted to mean that every Cohen and Levy reacts one
way and every Kelly or O'Brien, another.

Some of us were deeply touched, recently, by the fury of a
hurricane. From one of Long Island's parkways, I saw some
dozen boats washed up or smashed against the water's edge.
It was easy to imagine the sadness of the owners at losing
crafts to which they were warmly attached.

But on that same day I also saw a magnificent tree bowed
before the storm's fury and smitten beyond hope of restoration
. . . and my grief at this sight was far more deep and abiding.
I asked myself: "What rational basis is there for the intensity
of my feeling?" Only that I am a Jew—and as a Jew, the vision
of life coming to an end, the life of something good and beautiful and growing, means that a little bit of me dies too. For
all that lives within God's creation is part of me.

During World War II, a fellow officer at the Anzio beachhead in Italy argued with me about the Allied bombing of
the historic Cassino monastery: "How can we justify destroying a great work of art which took hundreds of years to create? Just to save a few lives of men who would eventually die
in our century?"

That captain was quite willing, perhaps, to die himself for
Cassino. But, for the Jew there is no question. Stones and
bricks are replaceable, man is not. No castle, no shrine, no
exquisite work of art is worth the life of one little infant!

I wonder how well we Americans heed the Biblical injunction in developing the pattern of our lives. A visitor from another planet, engaged in a sociological study of our country,
might be somewhat startled at the pride we exhibit in our
matchless mobility, our fast automobiles and broad highways,
when he learned that every twenty-five years we lose over one

million lives and cripple twenty-five million others at the wheel. Just think of it: a nation with the highest standard of living ever known, and with more trained minds than any people in human history—and yet willing to sacrifice one million human beings in twenty-five years. "Behold, I give you life and death, a blessing and a curse," declared Moses. "What do you choose?"

A few weeks ago I read a sermon by the Protestant chaplain of Sing Sing prison, strongly urging the abolition of capital punishment. "It is time," said the minister, "to introduce a Christian attitude toward the taking of human life, and to eliminate once and for all the Jewish Old Testament practice."

This is not the first Christian teacher to distort Jewish doctrine by singling out the most primitive practices of a people three thousand years ago and labeling these as "Jewish." Would this minister, I wonder, identify present-day Protestantism with savagery and barbarism because, not so long ago, devout church people burned innocent Salem women for the crime of witchcraft?

How ironic that the taking of human life be identified with Jewish teaching. Our friend from Ossining might ponder on the fact that no Buddhist country in the world countenances capital punishment. Israel, the only Jewish state, destroyed its executioner's equipment in 1950, when the nation was two years old. The taking of life as punishment is a practice which remains largely in Christian countries.

The Eichmann trial offered to the world a stark reminder of the cold indifference to human values on the part of those who held life in their hands. In 1938, and again in 1943, there were conferences called by our State Department and the British Foreign Office to handle "the refugee emergency." Newspaper editorials cried out for action. Two million Jews had already been destroyed. A Southern newspaper said: "Some of us are a little ashamed of our country." Two Jewish Congressmen—Celler and Dickstein—pleaded on the floor of the House of Representatives: "Appoint a commission; find some answer; find some room." And one British Foreign Office spokesman asked: "What would we do with a million Jews?"

At Carnegie Hall, in June, 1943, Edgar Ansel Mowrer told the audience: "I am certain that ways can be found to force the Nazis to stop the mass murder of Jews . . . I have no doubt that history will condemn us most severely for our failure . . . I often ask myself, what will I say to my grandchildren when they ask me, how was it possible to permit the murder of millions of innocent men, women, and children? We shall all live to carry the shame before future generations."

The past is history. Post-mortems offer some light, but not life.

For me, there is an unforgettable lesson in all this. Some Jews suggest that mankind has reached that sophisticated, enlightened stage of development when parochialism of a particular creed is obsolete. Why not embrace the unweighed faith of ethical culture, of religious humanism, or a distillation of the best in every faith, as in Bahai?

To me, the hope of mankind lies in a tenacious retention of that particular way of life known as Judaism—an attitude of mind which keeps affirming life, which tells and retells the simple truth that man, who can't create a single fingernail, has no business tampering with the life of a single human being. In our time, we have somehow turned away from the Age of Compassion and entered the Era of Callousness. But we Jews, who know the meaning of deprivation and death, have learned all the more fervently to say: *Lechayim.*

The world still needs the constant reminder of the Jew: *Thou shalt choose life!*

# Religion in the Affluent Society

JOHN K. GALBRAITH, in his brilliant and popular book, *The Affluent Society*, presents a strikingly novel thesis. He declares that our institutions and our value system are based on a society of scarcity, and are therefore outmoded and unsuited to a land of abundance, such as America.

As I read the development of this theme, I was struck by its relevance to the field of religion in general, and to the Jewish faith in particular.

What the good Harvard professor is saying is this: Throughout history the vast majority has always lived in abject poverty. Food, clothing, a roof over their heads—these were the primary problems that occupied their lives and energies.

Now, for the first time, some countries of the world—still only a very few, to be sure—have entered a new stage altogether. In these fortunate lands, the majority is reasonably secure. Only a fringe of the population worries about tomorrow's meals or rent. But, asks Professor Galbraith, have our social institutions kept pace with progress? No, they have not. Our cities are in the process of self-strangulation. Our crime rate is higher than ever. And our people, though better fed and clothed, are certainly no nearer to contentment. Something, says Dr. Galbraith, is clearly amiss.

This thesis is particularly provocative, it seems to me, in the realm of religious thought. Every historic faith was born out of the depths of poverty and want. In the Orient and in many other parts of the world the central theme of religion is suffering and the beggar is held up as a saint. In countries like Siam, even today, the Prime Minister and the King must give up so many days each year to be beggars in the streets.

The symbolism in Christianity is the stable, the humble dwelling at Nazareth. The Moslems emphasize the poverty and misery of Mohammed, the camel driver; Passover . . . slaves: "Let the poor enter"; Sukkot . . . "In huts dwelt our forefathers."

Study Jewish literature, which mirrors the life experience of our people, and you will find one central theme: poverty and hunger. Every story of Sholom Aleichem, of Peretz, tells the same tale. Sholom Aleichem's hero Tevye the Dairyman is immersed in the wretchedness of want. Most of the humor in Sholom Aleichem is of a wry, bittersweet type. And Peretz, too, depicts Jewish life as having as its two basic ingredients, *veitog und ziskeit,* pain and sweetness.

C. N. Bialik, the greatest Jewish poet of the twentieth century, was asked why everything he wrote was in a minor, melancholy key. He penned a poem, *"Meayin Yovoh Shiri"*— "Whence Comes My Song?" In it, Bialik describes his early childhood in a small Russian town. He lost his father when he was seven; his impoverished mother went to work before daybreak and did not return until after dark. On weekdays, Bialik never saw his mother and the sun in the skies at the same time. Before she left her home, she baked bread . . . and cried over her bitter lot. The mother's tears fell into the dough, and the bread baked with her tears entered the very bone and marrow of the child.

Israel Zangwill's hero in the East End of London (why do Jews always settle on the East End first—to be a little nearer Jerusalem?) is the "King of the Schnorrers." The whole concept of the *schnorrer* stems out of collective Jewish poverty.

Even in American Jewish literature this emphasis continues. To find pure goodness, saintliness, lofty character, you must look for it in hovels. The noble souls in Sholem Asch are the poorest piece-goods workers in the Norfolk Street basements. Once the hero becomes a prosperous manufacturer, he loses his humanity, his decency, and often his integrity. In *East*

*River* it is the *nouveaux-riches* waist manufacturers who, without souls and greedy for more gain, cause the tragedy of the Triangle Shirtwaist Company fire.

The family of Herman Wouk's *Marjorie Morningstar* seemed to possess fine qualities until they moved up the economic ladder to Central Park West. Myron Kaufmann's *Remember Me To God* describes a prosperous Jewish family in Boston's finest suburbs, and there isn't a decent person in the whole *mishpochah*.

A valid hero or heroine in a Jewish novel has got to be on the verge of bankruptcy or, at the very least, a Last Angry Doctor, whose fees are minimal or nonexistent.

This array of fictional characters is an accurate reflection of our moral and spiritual standards. Ancient Jewish tradition, and Christian value systems as well, exalt poverty as a glorious virtue. *Vayishman Yeshurun*—"When Israel waxed fat, it became corrupt." Or, again, "It is easier for a camel to go through the eye of a needle, than for a rich man to enter into the kingdom of God."

Can one be religious in an affluent society? What will happen to the milk of human kindness, to compassion, when there are not many ready beneficiaries? What do the old Sunday school heroes—the saints and sages who lived in tents, in caves, in musty cellars—mean to the child whose life is bounded by car pools, beach clubs, hot fudge sundaes, and generous allowances, all available without their lifting a finger?

We have somehow drifted along in the belief that the guiding moral and spiritual principles that served our grandfathers will do equally well for us. But do they, or do the old key phrases in our prayer books, written for the age of scarcity, leave us cold today?

Norman Cousins' biography of Dr. Albert Schweitzer portrays one of the rarest, most wonderful human beings on earth, a man who left comfort and ease behind him and chose instead to heal strangers in the jungle at Lambaréné. When I

describe Schweitzer's life to a young person—a world without bed sheets and pillowcases, without television, without
movies, without automobiles, motorboats, baseball games—
can I do it in such a way that the youngster can nevertheless
identify with this man, that he can say to himself, "That's the
kind of human being I would like to be"?

Those of us in synagogue and church who are seriously
concerned with the abiding values in life will have to devote
some of our mental energies to creating a spiritual climate
that can have meaning in our abundant society. But where do
we start?

Perhaps we should begin by taking a close look at this
affluence we're a part of. It exists in only a tiny segment of
the world. Two out of every three people on earth still earn
less than $100 a year, have only one meal a day, go to bed
hungry. Four out of five human beings never see a doctor
from birth to death. While our pharmaceutical firms produce
more wonder drugs than any of us can possibly use, tens of
millions of our fellow men writhe in pain, walk with crippled
limbs, lose their precious eyesight—simply because the drugs
they need so desperately are in New Brunswick or Indianap-
olis, not in Algiers, Calcutta, or Hong Kong.

Our first and most obvious task, therefore, is to help convince our fellow Americans (and are we ourselves fully convinced?) that we must share our God-given wealth, that we
dare not stand by unmoved while people anywhere are cold,
hungry, or sick.

What about the role of our particular faith in the abundant
society? I believe Judaism has enduring values for the world
of plenty. For despite our traditional exaltation of the poor,
we have rarely placed a premium on asceticism for its own
sake. Judaism has never demanded, as a tenet of faith, the
monastic denial of pleasures our world has to offer.

Remember Harry Golden's story about his mother's pet
phrase, "Enjoy, enjoy"? That word "enjoy" is, in a sense, a
Jewish watchword.

Judaism not only insists on marriage for all, it requires,

yes, *requires* that partners in marriage share in the physical aspects of marital life. The Bible tells us to use wine for religious occasions because "wine rejoices the heart of man." Our critics often deplore what they call our emphasis on this world. But a study of comparative religions makes it quite evident that the historic faiths conjured up dreams of a physical hereafter largely because, for the vast majority of people, life in this world had precious little to recommend it. Jews alone fashioned a code of life geared to this world alone.

*When civilization reaches the stage when most of mankind— the people of the Congo and Indonesia, the people of Afghanistan and Saudi Arabia—can share in the affluent society, Judaism may well reach out to become one of the dominant religions of this globe.*

But whether it does or not, those of us who have moved away from an economy of scarcity have an urgent need for a value system that will stand up in an age of plenty. For example, what creative uses shall we make of leisure? We are well on the way to a four-day week, a weekend that begins on Thursday afternoon. Will we use those newfound hours to broaden our minds, to add new dimensions of beauty to our lives? Will we now find time to cultivate one of the arts, to discover aesthetic fulfillment as painters, sculptors, poets, clarinetists, composers? Relieved of the overwhelming preoccupation with providing for our basic needs, will we generate the impetus that will move us a notch higher in the scale of civilization?

In the Prophets we read the story of Hannah, who prayed to God to grant her a son. When her prayers were answered and a son was born, Hannah named him Samuel, meaning "God has heard me," and she consecrated her son's life to the service of his Creator. Hannah was haunted all her life with the thought that everything—life's possessions, even life itself —is simply *borrowed from the Lord.*

And this phrase is the beacon of light and direction for the beneficiaries of the abundant society. Those of us who truly believe—not simply mouth the phrase, but understand deep in our hearts—that all we call our own is borrowed from the Lord, that every lease of which we are master is temporary, that the most blessed among us are but stewards of our earthly possessions, these are the men and women who have the answer of the Prophets.

# Who Is Responsible?

I AM ALWAYS SURPRISED at the number of people who still insist on taking the 22nd Chapter of Genesis—the epic tale of Abraham's willingness to offer his son, Isaac, as a sacrifice to God—quite literally. I firmly believe that to regard this story as history or biography is to miss the point entirely. To be understood, the story of the sacrifice on Mount Moriah must be seen as an exalted moral parable.

When we read the account of the episode on Mount Moriah, we must pass over the frightful aspects of human sacrifice and concentrate on what the Biblical author, indeed, what Jewish tradition, is saying to us.

Where is Mount Moriah? (To learn this is important for an understanding of the Bible's purpose.) Moriah, according to Jewish tradition, is Mount Zion, the hill that overlooks Jerusalem. Only a few months ago, together with thousands of pilgrims, my family walked up those slopes and stood on the spot where the ancient Temple of Solomon stood, at the site of King David's tomb. In Jewish tradition, this hilltop is the most sacred, most revered bit of soil on earth. Why is it holy? Not because King Solomon built the majestic sanctuary there. This spot was selected as a sanctuary because it had already been hallowed through Abraham's presence, through Abraham's act of sacrifice, and through Isaac's assent to the sacrifice.

If we probe deeply enough into the essence of the story, we will understand what Judaism has for us in the way of profound instruction.

Each of us has our own Mount Moriahs—ideas and ideals

which move us to great sacrifices. Indeed we are willing to give up the very things we cherish most, our loved ones, our possessions, in order to achieve our objectives.

It does not mean we reject or do not love the people or the things we are willing to sacrifice. A young man I know, who already has the responsibilities of a family, tells me he is about to enter medical school. What will happen to his children while he is not earning a livelihood? What about the burden on his wife? "This is my goal, my life's ambition," he answers. "Ultimately they too will benefit from my decision, but at all events, I can do no other. My loved ones must join me on my Mount Moriah."

But there is a second lesson that emerges from the story of Abraham's sacrifice.

A great decision has been made, a terrifying decision, with dire consequences. Whom does the Bible blame? Is this the act of a capricious, demanding Deity? No . . . Abraham, according to tradition, assumes full responsibility. Not even Sarah is told of his decision. There are times in life, says Abraham, when one man alone, in the solitude of his own soul, must search out all the choices, scan all the consequences, and say firmly: This is *my* decision; mine alone.

You remember the slogan on Harry Truman's desk in the White House: "The buck stops here!" The Berlin crisis, the atom bomb, the Marshall Plan, Korea—and no one else in the world to pass the buck to. This was Harry Truman's Mount Moriah.

The message of Abraham's sacrifice is timeless, but in a very real sense it is urgently timely in our own generation.

It is almost impossible, today, for an individual to act with any measure of independence. Some months ago, a Jewish professor of history, a Frenchman, sought an audience with the Pope to ask his help in eliminating anti-Jewish references in Catholic textbooks. Pope John XXIII, who happens to be the same age as his Jewish guest, smiled at his visitor and said softly: "You know, my dear professor, I'm not the boss around here. We have a team, and I must work through my associates."

The cynic may suggest that this infallible leader of half a billion human beings was merely evading a quick decision. Possibly this is so. But if a following of over 500 million people gives you power, it also imposes restraint. You may have half a billion people behind you, but you also have a fifth of the world's population on your shoulders, and an elaborate organization of associates with whom you must live and work harmoniously.

But if a man with so much authority feels the need to share responsibility, what about ordinary people like ourselves? Must we assume the full burden of our own decisions, whatever they may be?

The same question was posed in a great courtroom trial a few years ago, in Israel. Judge Landau, later the presiding judge in the Eichmann case, sat in judgment. A Jewish officer was charged with leading a raid on an Arab village and ordering the slaughter of a number of innocent Arab civilians. His defense was simple: "I am a soldier," he said. "I was simply obeying military orders to preserve the security of Israel."

Judge Landau's historic pronouncement goes to the very heart of the moral issue: *You, and you alone, are responsible for the moral consequences of your actions.*

At some point in our lives we all climb our own Mount Moriah. And when we do, we can no longer lean on friends, family, associates, or superiors. We each stand on Mount Moriah *alone,* and are judged alone in God's sight.

The structure of modern-day living makes it quite easy to avoid responsibility. The notion of group responsibility penetrates every facet of our lives. The business world has elaborate mechanisms of interlocking authority. In the political arena, we are frightened at the thought of one man alone making crucial decisions. We are comforted, somehow, in the thought that President Kennedy is counseling not only with his own soul but also with the National Security Council, as though the decisions of ten men are inevitably wiser than the instincts of one.

When I was three years old, my clothing caught fire. I was severely burned and for days I hovered between life and death. The decisions about whether to operate, whether to apply skin grafts, and a score of other medical considerations lay in the hands of one man, Dr. Henderson, in a village six hundred miles north of Toronto, Canada, where I lived. He was a country doctor, without a hospital, without an anesthetist, without laboratory assistants, without blood plasma. My young life was in his hands alone. I draw no medical moral from this episode. The fact that I am here today may be due more to the fact that God was good to me than to the skill of that one man alone. I cite this only to underscore the simple fact that the Dr. Hendersons are seldom called upon to make these awesome decisions any more. And there are fewer and fewer areas in which we must act in isolation from our colleagues.

Yet the fundamental lesson of religion remains the same: The basic moral decisions in life are ours alone. The temptations are greater, the escape hatches larger, and the counter-arguments a little more persuasive. But a human being still must look himself squarely in the mirror and say: "Not my team, not my company, not my country club . . . I am the one who sets the moral standards for myself!"

One way to measure the moral standards of a particular generation is to study its definition of courage. Who are the heroes of our age? Analyze, for example, the leading characters in the novels of Ernest Hemingway. Hemingway has much to say about courage. I dare say he reflects quite accurately the mood of our age. Hemingway's heroes, with the exception of *For Whom the Bell Tolls,* are possessed of remarkable *physical* courage. They are brave men . . . but without any particular purpose beyond adventure for its own sake. They battle not for any lofty goal, but for the zest of combat. The enemy is not ignorance, disease, or inhumanity, but the bull in the ring, or the sea and the storm.

The Jewish definition of courage suggests another kind of fortitude—the ability to stand up in a minority and be counted; the strength to be different when the majority prefers to perpetuate racial bias or cut corners in commerce; the honesty to face ourselves as we are, admitting our shortcomings without excuses and self-justification.

Arthur Miller wrote a moving play called, *All My Sons,* on this very theme. The "hero," Joe Keller, manufactures airplane parts during World War II. To increase his profit, he allows twenty-one defective cylinders to pass into production. Twenty-one planes crash; twenty-one young lives are lost. A trial is held, and in the course of it, Joe Keller succeeds in shifting the blame to his partner. How could *he* possibly be guilty of killing twenty-one young men . . . it must have been someone else.

But in the denouement of the play, Joe learns that his own son, also a flier, has taken his plane out on a suicide mission after hearing about the trial. Joe cannot understand what has driven his son to a dive-bomb death. "I guess to my boy those other fellows were all my sons," he says. Joe Keller ultimately takes his own life, still not understanding, still unable to face the moral consequences of his own behavior.

In our undramatic lives, we are often unaware of how frequently we shift responsibility to others. For example . . . the first *mitzvah* in Jewish life is mentioned in the same breath with the *Shema.* In every prayer book, Orthodox, Conservative, and Reform, the *Shema* is followed by the injunction: "Thou shalt teach them diligently unto thy children." It doesn't say: "Hire a teacher and let them know"; or "Send them to Sunday school and let them learn." The command reads, "*You* teach them; *you* instruct them; *you* inform them; *you* inspire them." Religion is not piano playing, or tap dancing, or tennis, cultivated by professional teachers you can hire. Religion is an outlook on life, an attitude of mind and heart nurtured in a setting of love and warmth and contentment of spirit which only the home can provide. If our children adore us—and what children, given the chance, do not idolize their parents—

they will almost of necessity embrace the values we cherish, and set their life's goals on the same wave length with our own.

It is always puzzling to meet someone who tells me: "I'm a modernist, I don't go too much for all those miracles in the Bible. Imagine Moses changing a stick into a snake; that's plain old-fashioned magic!" And that same modernist says to me: "Here is my child. Take him; repeat the right incantation over him; and transform him into a good and loyal Jew."

It seems to me that parents have an infinite capacity for self-deception. Ask a housewife what she puts into a cake, and she will list eggs, flour, salt, sugar, shortening. Ask her what she, as a mother, puts into her children, and she will list half a dozen ingredients that really aren't there. But no matter how we fool ourselves, we can't get more out than we put in. Being a parent is a full-time job. Being a Jewish parent should entitle one to time and a half for overtime. Unless there is some deliberateness in Jewish parenthood, some thoughtful, conscientious planning, the children we rear will not be the adults we expect them to be.

All of us have our calls to sacrifice, the insistent demands reminding us that everything worthwhile in life entails a giv-ing of ourselves. If, like Abraham, we find the courage to see ourselves as we are and assume responsibility for what we do, our own Mount Moriahs can also be personal sanctuaries worthy of the blessing of God.

# Solitude and Society:
# Two Ways to God

THERE IS NOTHING more intriguing than a paradox. For
a paradox suggests that truth, like the Roman god Janus, has
two faces. Is it really possible for a statement to contain an
inner contradiction, yet to be valid none the less? Amusing or
entertaining, yes; diverting, yes. But not really true. For in an
orderly universe, black is black and white is white, and neither
is a combination of the two.

But the genius of paradox—and its mystery—is that it
often represents a higher form of truth than a simple, unadorned statement of fact. The rearing of children, for example, offers most parents an exquisite combination of pain
and joy. There is no simple formula for helping our once-
helpless young become mature human beings—independent
and apart, yet in so many ways eternally bound to us. Rabbi
Milton Steinberg called it the art of letting go and holding on
at the same time—"embracing with open arms." In the same
way, does not happiness and self-realization often come when
we lose ourselves completely in a thought, a passage of music,
a person, an all-absorbing cause? The very word, ecstasy,
suggests that being beside ourselves or outside ourselves is the
most satisfying way of being ourselves.

Judaism has always been enamored of paradoxes. One
familiar Jewish story, which must have antecedents as far
back as the wilderness of Sinai, tells of a rabbi who arbitrated
a dispute. After hearing the first man, the rabbi assured him
that justice was on his side. When the second had presented
his case, the rabbi told him, "You are also right." And when

the rabbi's wife called him to task for his inconsistency, he shook his head: "You are right too."

To me, one of the attractions of Judaism lies in its modest recognition that we don't have all the answers. Religion, by definition, is supposed to deal with certainties. We come to it with our problems and we expect well-packaged solutions. Yet Judaism is full of "We don't know" and "We can never know." A key phrase, oft repeated in Jewish tradition, is "perplexity." We can only inch our way toward certainties.

A nineteenth-century rabbi, lecturing to his seminary students about their prospective role as leaders, told a parable about some youthful travelers who lost their way in a thick forest. After wandering for days, the desperate group met an old man. Immensely relieved, they asked him to lead them out of the woods. He responded with a sigh: "You have been perplexed about the way out for just a few days. I've been perplexed for years. How can *I* lead the way?"

There was little comfort for the neophyte rabbis in their master's tale. Were they destined, then, to become leaders dim of vision, the blind, taking it upon themselves to lead the blind? But Judaism would say: Who is finite man, with his limited vision and his brief life span, to speak of anything but *approximate* truth and *tentative* explanations? Better a hesitant, partial truth than a dogmatic untruth.

One who views Judaism from afar will be struck by this amazing inconsistency: The Jewish religion has evolved an elaborate ritual to cover everything a man ought or ought not to *do* during every waking moment, even every sleeping moment, of life. But it is distinctly vague and uncertain about what a man ought or ought not to *believe*. Judaism says: *Act* justly, *give* freely, *practice* kindness. But if someone asks why —demands to be told the philosophic and theological grounds for such behavior—the answer is that we have not yet discovered the final answers to the ultimate problems of human existence. And while we are waiting for the theologians and the philosophers to come up with these answers, we must live decently and treat our neighbors kindly.

Permeating Jewish law, from the Bible, the ancient Talmud, through the medieval codes and later responsa (books of rabbinic decisions) is the phenomenon of two opinions. Is every word of the Bible true? Its pages abound in contradictions. How is God to be worshiped? The priests of the Temple present a detailed list of burnt offerings, meal offerings, sin offerings, while the prophets tell us: "What need I of offerings, saith the Lord . . . help the poor, feed the hungry, clothe the naked."

The name of the first Talmudic rabbi, Hillel, is familiar to most of us. Less known is Shammai, who invariably disagreed with his colleague, so that a thousand rabbis who came after them were divided into sharply defined schools of thought. Is the Book of Job a true story or an allegory? Is there physical immortality? For every question there are two equally acceptable, though contradictory, opinions.

Judaism's way to God, then, is not a single-lane road, but a broad highway. What is important is not that we all travel the same path but that we all head in the same direction. The rabbis and sages and teachers all agree on man's responsibility to his fellow man, man's obligation to make a heaven on his earth. But on the nature of the other heaven, on the nature of God, we can only agree, says the greatest mind in all Jewish thought, Moses Maimonides, on what they are *not*. God is not physical; He is not finite as we are.

Today, too, we find some of the outstanding leaders of Jewish thought in sharp disagreement with one another on such basic issues as the nature of salvation, or what moderns call self-fulfillment and self-realization. How do we achieve a sense of completion?

Rabbi Abraham Joshua Heschel, whose roots are deep in the Hasidic tradition, stresses what he calls "inwardness." He sees the goal of man in the lonely striving for perfect communion with God. "Better a prayer without a synagogue than a synagogue without a prayer," Rabbi Heschel writes. He would agree completely with the answer of a Hasidic rabbi who was asked why virtuous men seem less eager to convert others to their ways than are sinners in enlisting companions in evil. "The good man," explained the rabbi, "walks in light and is not afraid to walk alone; but the sinner walks in darkness and therefore prefers company."

Heschel tells us that though we need to contemplate nature in order to perceive the majesty and awe of Creation and the Creator, "an encounter with the ineffable" is attained only when we draw a cloak around ourselves, removing all distraction. Just as the artist must search in solitude for his own way to express, in some degree, the inexpressible, so does man come closest to God when he is alone. Such is Professor Heschel's eloquent exposition of the way to God. But is it the authentic  voice in Judaism?

Certainly Heschel is *an* authentic voice of our people. But in another stream of contemporary Jewish thought we find the equally appealing views of Professor Mordecai M. Kaplan. Both men are impatient with each other, an impatience which borders on intolerance. For, as the Talmud says, nothing is quite as heated as the atmosphere surrounding scholars in dispute.

Dr. Kaplan's brilliant classic, *Judaism as a Civilization,* holds that for the Jew, God is only to be found through His people. "Only through interaction with his group can the individual achieve personality and self-fulfillment, or salvation."

Kaplan can find much in Jewish tradition to support his view. The gregariousness which has marked Jewish life has its origins in our views of the universe, our theology. The intensity of Jewish social relationships and the countless ways in which the community enters into the life of the individual have long been noted by the social historian. In some ethnic traditions, nothing is more sacred than privacy. In Judaism, however, a lock on the door is unthinkable: "Keep thy doors open," says the Talmud. "Separate not thyself from the community."

Can we explain all this entirely in terms of social forces— as an outgrowth of ghetto living? Was this "clannishness" simply a response to the threat of attack, as in the days of the American frontier?

I don't think this is the whole explanation. Perhaps part of the answer is that Judaism boasts the longest continuing tradition in Western culture. Jews have always been enthralled with the idea of family transmission. We are the only modern people to preserve the ancient tribal quality of our group. In today's vocabulary the word, tribal, has an unpleasant ring—for no unit smaller than a nation is respectable. But Judaism has never been able to separate family from faith, family from group, family from history. It is this intoxication with history that has led the Jew to accept the idea that he is an inseparable part of a whole—past, present, and future.

What, then, is the ideal way to God in Judaism? There are enough alternatives for every man to make his own choice. Perhaps there will never be one religion, one universal spiritual philosophy that satisfies us all. Some of us may become attuned with the Infinite only when our spirits interlock with those of other human beings. We need a *minyan*, the warmth of fellowship, a communion with other souls in order to sense a communion with the divine. Others of us may experience an inner peace and a feeling of the sublime when we are alone, requiring only the companionship of God's other handiwork —a shady tree at river's edge, the quietness of a secluded hilltop, the flight of sure-winged wild geese toward a rendezvous with the sunshine.

Dare we dogmatize, then, knowing but an infinitesimal part of all there is to know, and speaking to the hearts and minds of all manner of human beings? Our master and teacher Abraham Joshua Heschel is right when he bids us seek solitude and calls on us to "stand still and see God" in the mystery of Creation. And our master and teacher Mordecai Menahem Kaplan is surely speaking the truth when he tells us that we may best search for fulfillment in the society of those who share our hopes and destiny. And if you ask me how both can be right. I guess that you, too, are not altogether wrong.

# Mourning and Meaning

"CALL NO MAN DEAD," says the Talmud, "whose children continue his works." These words explain a great deal about the ceremonials traditional to death in a Jewish household. For in Judaism, even mourning is designed to give meaning to life—to reconcile the living to the finality of parting and to turn their thoughts and actions toward the world of the living.

I differentiate between mourning in Judaism and mourning in other faiths because the Jewish religion, except for a few brief periods in its development, has never held out to its adherents the promise of a resurrection and an afterlife. As Claude G. Montefiore points out in his brilliant introduction to A *Rabbinic Anthology,* classical Judaism is without a single reference to a possible reunion among loved ones in a hereafter. "Our generation goeth, and another cometh," we find written in Ecclesiastes. And the parting between them, when the time has come, is permanent and forever.

And so Judaism has fashioned mourning into a process for healing those devastated by their loss—a set of rituals that combine homage to the dead with tenderness and concern for the living. By thus describing and circumscribing the requirements of mourning, Judaism permits, indeed encourages, the mourners to turn without guilt to the sweetness of life.

More than anything else, Judaism stresses the normalcy of death. It is entirely natural for a man's life to have its limits, as does every other living thing. There is a sublime symmetry about the cycle of gestation, birth, growth, decline, and death. And if living is an art, dying too demands aesthetic perspective. Our wisest thinkers, our finest writers have always recognized in the dignity of death a kind of majestic beauty.

In today's complex and impersonal world, the *Hevrah Kadisha*, the Jewish community's volunteer burial society, has virtually disappeared. Much akin to the volunteer fire departments known to so many small towns in this country, the *Hevrah Kadisha* combines a sense of civic duty with an element of sociability. It was a mark of distinction to be a member of this group and to fulfill with real personal involvement those functions now carried on by the commercial funeral chapel.

It was the *Hevrah Kadisha* that was charged with guarding the democracy of death—another mourning custom unique to Judaism. The Jewish funeral was designed to emphasize the equality in God's eyes of rich and poor, high and low, hence no competitive ostentation was permitted. Whatever his station, the traditional Jew is buried in the same simple garb and the same unadorned coffin. Theoretically, a cortege passing in the street would give no hint of any earthly distinctions of wealth or class, but simply indicate that a child of God has passed away.

The most praiseworthy *mitzvah* (sacred duty) in Judaism is called *Seudat Havraah*, the preparation of a meal for a family returning from the cemetery. As these words suggest, it is the obligation of friends and neighbors to nourish the bereaved and bring them back to health. The emphasis is on the continuation of life and, as with many other Jewish customs, food symbolizes our warmth and concern.

To me there is a rich symbolism in the table, which I associate with the life-style of the traditional Jewish family. Today, when I visit a bereaved home, I generally find the family scattered, each in his own room. But in bygone days, and in more old-fashioned households, the entire group of mourners—babies, children, cousins, uncles and aunts, parents and grandparents—would all be clustered around the kitchen or dining-room table, sipping tea or coffee, needing, in their

grief, the warmth of one another's presence, and feeling the
comfort and support of the family united.

Perhaps the gathering of the clan around the kitchen table
—in joy as well as sorrow, for happiness as well as tragedy
deserved to be shared—reflects a way of life typical of a
lower economic class and an immigrant society. If that is
so, we have paid quite a price for our acceptance into the
native middle classes.

The mourner's prayer, the *Kaddish,* whose words are Ara-
maic, the language of the Talmud, the New Testament, and
parts of the Book of Daniel, makes no reference to death.
Its message is an extension of the opening words, "Magnified
and Sanctified is the name of the Lord." We do not know its
composer, nor what inspiration led to the use of this prayer,
originally chanted as a kind of apostrophe at the end of a
study session, to comfort the bereaved. But there is a stately
grandeur to the cadence of the *Kaddish,* like the basso pro-
fundo passages in Handel's Hallelujah Chorus, evoking, I
think, a very special sense of awe that chills and ennobles at
the same time.

The Hebrew word for funeral is *l'vayah,* which means
"accompaniment." It was the custom, in times past, for the
family and friends of the deceased to *walk* with measured
pace behind the coffin to its final resting place, in a kind of
personal leave-taking far removed from the hectic, perfunctory
respects we all too often pay today. And this procession, too,
by its very depth of personal involvement, served to liberate
the living for life.

I don't want to suggest that all Jewish mourning practices
have been uniformly inspirational or uplifting. Over the centuries, a great many superstitions current in the areas where
Jews have lived became part of the Jewish folkways as well.
As time passed there were many within the Jewish community
itself who failed to distinguish between essential Jewish ritual
and pagan encrustations. One such practice, described in
Solomon Maimon's autobiography, was the medieval custom
of measuring the grave of a loved one and donating to the

synagogue candles equal in length to the grave's circumference. Just where this rite originated is unknown, but certainly there is nothing in Jewish tradition to sanction it, and similar death rites were frequently denounced as pagan by the Biblical prophets.

Modern Judaism has succeeded in shedding many of these fringe observances—but even today we find some firmly entrenched. Some years ago a woman asked me to conduct a funeral service for her husband. "Rabbi," she warned me, "we are not superstitious—so we don't want such things as *Kaddish*." But when I visited her home I found all the mirrors covered with sheets, a custom born of the pagan fear that spirits who could see their reflections in the mirror would not willingly leave the home of the deceased! We moderns seem more ready to give up the meaningful rituals of comfort and sustenance than the senseless accouterments of ignorance and fear.

I sense, for instance, the imminent disappearance of the *Shivah*, the traditional requirement that all the immediate relatives in mourning remain together under one roof for several days and receive those who would share their grief. I think the death of this custom will mark the end of one more cementing force in family life. It is good for brothers and sisters whose link with one another has just been severed to be reunited in this kind of family ritual. When a second parent dies, we cease to be children for the first time in our lives. What better way to reorient ourselves to the demands of our newborn maturity than with one lingering bow to our role as offspring, in the company of those who must always and forever view us in that light.

The demands of modern living somehow do not permit a long recess. There are too many pressures, from the office, from school, from outside obligations. We can manage to get away for ten-day cruises or extensive jaunts into the country; but the exigencies of old-fashioned mourning seem unbearable. When I suggest to a bereaved family that they may want to remain together for a short time, I am sometimes greeted

by a look of sheer terror. The thought of being closeted together, brothers and sisters—and their spouses—for a pro-
tracted period casts a greater pall than the loss of a loved
one. We have so fragmentized our lives that there is nothing
left of "that old clan of mine."

Yet in our tradition the true immortality of parents rests
in their children—their attachment to one another, and to the
values they learned at their parents' knees. When a child
fulfills the ageless obligation of pronouncing the *Kaddish*, he
affirms that the God of his fathers is his God and that the
ideals of his parents have not perished with their passing.
How hollow is the comfort of physical rebirth compared to
the contemplation that all that has made our own lives meaningful—the spirit of our being—will continue in those who come
after us.

This, then, is the true immortality—and the comfort that
reaches in equal measure to the dying and to those they leave
behind. This is the message that Jewish mourning seeks to
impart.

That is why I am so hesitant about letting go of these
ancient rituals, evolved and tested over so many centuries.
Certainly we must not cherish perfunctory rites, carried on
in an unthinking, mechanical fashion. But neither must we
become allergic to a prescribed duty merely *because* it is
prescribed. The age-old tradition of *Yahrzeit*, beckoning the
family to a remembrance of parent or grandparent at the synagogue, has the profound spiritual purpose of saying to friends
and community that the heritage of our family is precious to
us. It has the even more profound purpose of reminding our
children that something of our parents and our grandparents
remains very much alive in us all.

Mourning has meaning as a sublime acknowledgment of
the divine rhythm of life, which makes the roses bloom and
fade away, but keeps their fragrance fresh in our minds
forever.

# Bar Mitzvah in Our Time: Uses and Abuses

NOTHING TRIES the soul of a rabbi more than the vulgar ostentation that mars certain Bar Mitzvah celebrations. Indeed, I have often been tempted to agree with those who would abolish Bar Mitzvah rites altogether because of these abuses. A glaring example came to my attention a short time ago, when the mother of a thirteen-year-old boy invited to one of these elaborate affairs was warned that her son was expected to wear a tuxedo. She demurred at the suggestion of formal attire for a boy barely five feet tall, and her hostess declared indignantly: "It costs us twenty-five dollars a plate to invite your Jeffrey, and we're having a ten-piece band. The least you can do is see to it that he comes properly dressed!"

I must confess that when I see a Bar Mitzvah boy whose skill at the twist and the cha-cha far exceeds his proficiency in Hebrew, I think there may be something to be said for the "abolition movement."

But it is only a momentary mood. One might as well eliminate college education because of the excesses that mark some graduation festivities, or suggest that Christians abandon Christmas because of the vulgarities of the office party. In all of these instances, constructive criticism must address itself to the abuse, not to the celebration itself.

For the Bar Mitzvah, marked in a meaningful, dignified way is, I submit, a stroke of genius in Judaism. It contributes to something precious and indispensable—the preservation of individuality.

A Christian education magazine, a number of years ago, pointed with some envy to this Jewish custom of singling out one individual in the congregation with an elaborate ritual highlighting his unique role in the congregational family. On that occasion he is not part of a class or part of a group; he stands alone, in a one-to-one relationship with the entire synagogue.

At no other time in our lives does a man enjoy a corresponding sense of his own worth. No one can recall the celebrations following his birth. And school recognition is necessarily a mass celebration: the most one can hope is that the presiding officer will call the names without mumbling as we ascend the graduation platform. Even in the marriage rite, one is merged with another, and the two are submerged in the blur of the wedding party. And as for the "last rites" . . .

Only the Bar Mitzvah singles each individual out. All eyes are on this one boy; all family preparations for months previous to the big event focus on him alone. And when the young man is called to the Torah, he knows as he stands before the Ark, that he truly counts in the eyes of man and God.

There is an awesomeness to the occasion as a tender youth says to himself: "I, Joseph, son of Jacob, assume responsibility for all my deeds henceforth and forever more." But there is also immeasurable comfort and strength in the knowledge that the world regards him as a responsible human being.

I am convinced that there is a link between the mushrooming rate of emotional disorder in our society and the decline of the individual in our culture. Dr. Karl Menninger, one of our most gifted psychiatrists, writes with pride of the following tribute to his profession from an experienced chaplain: "You seem to have a belief in the importance and the dignity of the individual human being. It is an assumption, of course, which you seem to make with a dedicated faith, that every individual is worth helping. You seem to believe that each individual has capacities for being destructive and capacities for being constructive and creative." Dr. Menninger has reason to be proud, for what the chaplain has described is not a common trait in our culture.

The counseling pastor shares with the counseling psychologist this simple principle: A person who has lost his way in the world must be made to feel that he counts, that he is a precious human being, worthy of attention. (Remember the stark tragedy in the climax of Arthur Miller's *Death of a Salesman*: the graveside scene when Willy Loman's widow cries out: "If only someone had paid him attention!")

Such a posture, pastoral or clinical, cannot be staged. The clergyman or the doctor must say to himself: "The suffering human being who sits before me is a child of God, with infinite capacities for goodness and for fulfillment as a human being."

It may seem a far cry from the festive mood of the Bar Mitzvah celebration to the sober counseling in a rabbi's study. But both moods represent profound insights into the mechanism of the human heart. The individual's healthy respect for himself, which is threatened in so many ways as he grows to maturity—by a universe of endless space, unknown and frightening, by the impersonal juggernaut of industrial structure, by political states in which the voice of the individual is constantly diminished—this positive force needs every bit of sustaining help a civilized society can offer.

At a Bar Mitzvah ceremony I recently witnessed in a Rio de Janeiro synagogue, six hundred congregants rose as the boy was "summoned to the Torah." Their standing tribute silently communicated itself to him, and added cubits to his own precious self-regard.

So, even when some Bar Mitzvah festivities are tawdry and lacking in good taste, there is still room for charity. Like the Hasidic rabbi I am so fond of quoting, who could see good even in the earthiest of God's creatures, I find some reassurance even in an abused occasion whose function is to tell a young man in the tender years of his groping adolescence: In our eyes, you are important!

# *I Still Believe in Man*

# I Still Believe in Man

THE SUMMER OF 1936 was not a good tourist season in the Holy Land. It was the year of the Arab riots. But my wife and I, youthfully blind to all danger, traveled the mined and sniper-ridden highways of Palestine. Atop the bus to Jerusalem, a British soldier rode leaning against his machine gun; inside the bus a second driver sat close to the wheel, ready to take over in case the driver was hit while negotiating the hairpin curves of the Judean hills.

Yet my most vivid memories of this first of nine pilgrimages to Israel are filled with happy moments in the company of extraordinary people.

We spent some time in the study of the poet laureate of Hebrew literature, Dr. Saul Tchernichowsky. The sign on his front door read: LITERARY HOURS 10 to 12; MEDICAL HOURS 2 to 4. He took care of poetry in the morning and pain in the afternoon. At the time of our visit, the poet-doctor was in his middle sixties. He wore a florid walrus mustache and his bright eyes flashed with life. On our arrival, he shook my hand, then greeted my wife and held her hand during the entire hour we stayed with him. In that austere study, which served both the poet and the medical practitioner, I repeated to myself over and over again those wonderful lines:

> Laugh at all my dreams, my dearest,
> Laugh, but I repeat anew:
> That I still believe in Man,
> As I still believe in you. . . .

Leaving that peaceful sanctum for the unpeaceful world that surrounded it, it was not easy to retain the spirit of eternal hope the poet engendered. The entire story of mankind, it seems to me, is a record of a continuing tension between the poetic and the prosaic—between lofty ideals and mundane reality.

In Judaism this sense of tension has been maintained at fever pitch for over three thousand years. It is an inner conflict that marked the very beginning of Jewish experience. Linked almost in one breath with the exhilaration of Sinai, and Moses' vision of a new morality, is the story of the Golden Calf. The reader asks himself: What kind of people was this, on the one hand deemed worthy of the Ten Commandments, yet primitive enough to make a god out of golden earrings? Spiritual greatness and abysmal superstition, side by side—thus the tension began.

Look at the period which produced many of the prophetic visions—the dreams of a time when "nation would not lift up sword against nation; neither would they learn war any more," and the gentle reminder, "What doth the Lord require of thee, only to do justice, love mercy and walk humbly with thy God." On the whole, it was an era of flagrant human exploitation, constant reversion to idol worship, feverish pursuit of material pleasures. What a chasm between the poetry of the prophet and the sordid facts of life.

But the dream somehow persisted, reinforced with the passage of the centuries. Three times a week for countless generations Jews read their Bibles in the synagogue, introducing their reading with the fateful blessing: "Thou hast chosen us." These words were never spoken in arrogance. By envisioning themselves in this special role, the Jews imposed upon themselves virtually superhuman moral demands and ethical expectations.

The parable of the two princes is a favorite theme in Judaism: It tells of a king who gave each of his two sons a field to tend. One prince was lazy and mused idly while his field lay neglected; the second was industrious—he planted well and nurtured the trees that grew until he had a fine orchard. But one day this industrious son decided to cut down the trees he had tended so carefully. The king was furious and punished the young prince severely. Whereupon the latter complained: Why am I punished when my field is no different from that of my lazy brother?

The people of Israel, says the parable, are like the industrious prince. These who know the right must suffer the consequences of doing wrong in the face of such knowledge.

So successfully did the Jews pursue this image of themselves that the entire world accepted it at face value. The Jewish community came to be weighed on a judgment scale different from other peoples'.

In our time this double standard is clearly seen in connection with the Arab refugees. Time and time again, in ancient times and modern, men and women have been made homeless by relentless forces of history. The American Indian pushed off his land as the pioneers pressed westward is only one of a thousand similar examples in every part of the world. In the years following World War II, as new nations were born and old ones reborn, the stream of refugees grew—in India, Pakistan, Poland, Red China, Tibet. We regarded these unfortunates pouring into Hong Kong, Calcutta, Karachi as human problems, the responsibility of humanity as a whole. Of course, many selfless people have worked to alleviate the suffering. I will never forget that handful of dedicated men and women in the tiny British colony of Hong Kong who have taken upon themselves the burden of salvaging over a million fellow human beings. But always, and rightly so, these efforts represent a response to the *need*, not a guilt about the impersonal political forces that produced the need. When I visited Dr. Radhakrishnan, the wise, scholarly president of India, he spoke with sadness and compassion about the human misery so widespread in Asia. But there was no word of self-criticism in connection with the dispossessed Moslems of his own new state.

The Arab refugees, on the other hand—whose plight grew out of the desperate war launched by the Arab League in an effort to thwart the UN partition vote—are somehow regarded as a burden on Israel's conscience. Voices strangely silent about other resettlement problems clamor loudly for Israel to take back all the Arabs who fled her borders in 1948, together with all the hundreds of thousands of children, many now almost grown, who were born in the refugee camps. And oddly enough, the Israelis themselves readily affirm a measure of responsibility for the Arab refugees, offering payments and restitution as part of a permanent peace treaty with the Arab countries.

In Israel a group known as *Ihud,* headed by Professors Martin Buber and Ernst Simon, whose founders included Dr. Judah Magnes, first president of Hebrew University, and Henrietta Szold, creator of Hadassah, agitate constantly for "peace and justice in our relations with the Arabs." I can think of no counterpart for such a group anywhere in the world except, perhaps, some prewar pro-India organizations in Great Britain. I have heard of no Bombay or Calcutta groups which demand justice for the Pakistanis; and even in our own country, organizations working to restore some measure of dignity to the American Indian can barely summon the support of a corporal's guard.

Israel—the people and the nation—is judged by more rigorous standards. There is little patience with human frailties or national shortcomings, if the humans happen to be Jews, and the nation, Israel. And the criticisms come as loudly from Jews as from non-Jews over Israel's failure to grant rights to the non-Orthodox, its rigid military supervision of its Arab minority, and those other admitted weaknesses of the new state.

Even the prosaic aspects of everyday living in Israel seem to give us pause. Those who visit the country for the first time expect to find themselves in a "thousand-and-one-nights" land with idyllic Biblical flavor. They are shocked at the noisy sidewalk cafes, the street peddlers, the bustle and cacophony. Where are the sounds of angels singing as they flutter through the skies that once looked down on Isaiah and Micah, Elijah and King Solomon? Why is there no blare of messianic trumpets? What's become of the blissful serenity of David's green pastures?

These great expectations, on every level from the most spiritual to the most mundane, impose a tremendous burden on the fledgling state. By definition, a nation has only one *raison d'être*, the welfare of its own citizens. But Israel from its inception envisioned itself in a much broader light.

For one thing, the country has assumed responsibility for gathering in all homeless Jews wherever they may be. Israel is the only country in the world whose population consists primarily of survivors. There is a phrase in the Bible that really should be incorporated in its national coat of arms. It reads: "By the skin of our teeth."

"Come in, we'll make room for you!" the new state says to Jews everywhere, especially those who are suffering oppression. And while none of Israel's statesmen thinks seriously of territorial expansion, it is easy to understand why its enemies are worried about unspoken plans. There is little rationality, given present limitations of space and supplies, in Ben-Gurion's invitation to two million Russian Jews. "How will we find room? By use of a time-honored device—another miracle!"

The self-appointment of Israel's leaders as spokesmen for Jews everywhere often annoys Jews in other parts of the free world. I shared the irritation of many other Americans, for example, when the Israeli Government made official representations to Great Britain and the United States over the synagogue desecrations in 1960. Who asked them to speak for us? Leaders of American Jewry have repeatedly called the Prime Minister to task over his habit of speaking "in behalf of world Jewry." I doubt, however, that "BG" will ever curb this habit despite his many amiable reassurances. His response is that of Jeremiah: "It is in my very bowels, and I must cry out." It may irritate his Jewish friends and alienate his supporters, but such is his vision of Israel, and it will not be denied.

Israel also sees itself as "a light unto the nations." What

a soaring ambition that is. Most new nations would be content with making certain its own roots are firm. Surely that is goal enough for one frontier generation. Not so the starry-eyed Israelis. Within a decade of its birth, the new state launched an Israel aid-to-the-underprivileged program. Does not the Talmud say: even the penniless must disburse alms?

The outpouring of Israel's limited resources to help the still newer nations of Asia and Africa join the twentieth century stands among the most dramatic of modern man's affirmations in behalf of his fellows. Golda Meir, the young state's foreign minister, explained her country's position to the United Nations with great passion: "Because Western man waited for centuries before coming into the atomic age," she declared, "does not mean that the peoples of Asia and Africa will have to wait patiently." And so the Israelis dispatch their finest men, the fruits of sacrificial training, to Ghana and the Congo, to Burma and Malaya, to help these new states pick themselves up by their boot straps as Israel has done—sharing precious know-how, training administrators, teaching the youth, coaxing new industries into being, helping young nurses and doctors gain valuable skills. The finest gift any nation, any people, can offer is this—to give of themselves.

During one of my recent visits to Israel I introduced Dr. Norman Vincent Peale to David Ben-Gurion. As we sat in the Prime Minister's office, the two men reached out to know one another.

"I understand you are a successful writer. What do you write about, Dr. Peale?"

The popular American minister made some brief reference to "positive thinking."

"What's positive thinking?"

Dr. Peale smiled. "If you have faith in yourself, faith in your fellow man and faith in God—that's 'positive thinking.'"

The Premier raised his palm, and with a gesture typical of Talmudic disputation, shrugged: "*That's* 'positive thinking'? Ah, we Jews thought of it a thousand years ago!"

Only one word captures the quality of this faith—Ben-

Gurion's favorite word—messianic: "It shall come to pass, in the end of days . . ."

Most of us regard this term as otherworldly, a touch of the apocalyptic. But the messianic impulse in Judaism is essentially no more—and no less—than a belief in the inevitability of perfection. Some day this world of ours will be perfect—without envy, greed, hatred, injustice. When that day will come we do not know, but come it will. And each of us can "hasten the footsteps of the Messiah" by building our own little world, our family, our community and our country, in the prophetic image.

That is why our Jewish tradition teaches that there must be no conflict between individual aspiration and universal hope, national fulfillment and international realization.

In this perspective we all would do well to combine within ourselves an impatient vision of the future and a patient understanding of the present. And it seems to me that Israel, especially, deserves this patience.

The mundane Israel is, of course, subject to the same blemishes and shortcomings of all human enterprises: disunity in politics, intolerance in matters of faith, severity toward its non-Jewish minority. But to characterize these faults as human is not to excuse or explain, merely to seek suspension of judgment. The first Chief Rabbi of modern Palestine, Abraham Kook, reminded his people that when the ancient Temple of Solomon was being built carpenters and masons with soiled hands and muddy sandals tracked dirt into the Holy of Holies. But when the temple was complete, it took on all the aspects of a sanctuary.

One last thought: Those superficial observers of Israel's spectacular growth who comment cynically on the "brilliant fund-raising" behind the hundreds of millions of dollars poured into this effort by American Jews miss the mark entirely. A man gives not to an appeal but to a cause, to an idea. And he gives tremendously only to a tremendous idea, such as a storm-tossed people in a land redeemed. When I share with free Jews everywhere in this miraculous enterprise, I add inches to the stature of my people and, at the same time, I help all mankind grow tall.

The poet Tchernichowsky, whose lines I quoted at the beginning of these observations, wrote in that same lovely poem:

> Let the time be dark with hatred,
> I believe in years beyond,
> Love at last shall bind the people
> In an everlasting bond.

# Shadows in the East

MY JOURNEY TO THE Soviet Union, in the summer of 1956, was a kind of pilgrimage to "the land of my fathers." My parents were born in the Ukraine, near the city of Kiev and, as far as I know, all my ancestors for the past several hundred years had their roots not far from Odessa. I say "land of my fathers" without apology, for modern Judaism derives much of its vitality from the great academies, the scholars, poets, dreamers, and political visionaries who preserved and enhanced Jewish values and traditions in the Jewish villages of Russia and Poland.

My rabbinic colleagues and I went to Russia for two reasons: to see and to be seen. With much trepidation—for even in 1956 touring Russia was still a rare thing—we flew to Moscow to check on the persistent rumors that a new spirit of religious freedom had been detected in the Soviet Union. Reports had it that the Jewish community was breathing more easily; that synagogues were open and flourishing and that facilities for Passover observance and the purchase of kosher foods were more readily available. Was there any truth to these stories?

We went too, to be seen, to communicate with the isolated two and a half million Jews of Russia, out of contact with their coreligionists for four decades. In a way it was like visiting another planet. There was a sense of unreality in talking with Jews who seemed to have been living in a state of suspended animation. They asked questions about Jewish leaders long dead and religious life long forgotten, as though they had not read a newspaper or a magazine in a quarter of a century.

Our first penetration of the Iron Curtain was at the airport in Riga, Latvia. As we made our way into the dining room, a four-piece string quartet spiritedly played a Jewish song: "Rozhinkes mit Mandlen." Who, we wondered, instructed the band to play that tune? And what prompted the leader to respond to our *Bolshoi spaseebo* (thank you very much), with the Hebrew words *Sholom aleichem* (peace unto you)?

One of the first Jews who greeted us when we entered a synagogue was an old man with a flowing beard, who spoke to us in Yiddish. "Are you Jewish, are you from America?" And then, his face not more than six inches from mine, *"Boruch atah Adonoy . . .* Praised art Thou O Lord God who has sustained us and kept us alive to this glorious day!"

In the Leningrad Synagogue, Rabbi Israel Mowshowitz began with the Biblical words: "I seek my brethren." The women, high in the gallery, began to applaud, and when the head of the congregation told them that it was unseemly to clap hands on the Sabbath in a house of God, they responded by applauding louder and stamping their feet to show us how they felt.

People have asked me over and over again: "Were you able to see what you wanted to in the Soviet Union?" Technically, the answer is yes. Our travel was not formally restricted. We could walk through the street, take a subway train, a bus, or a taxi and go anywhere in Moscow or Leningrad. But where can you go if you don't even know where you are? There were no maps of the city, no guide books, no street directories, no phone books. Imagine being in a hotel near New York's Times Square and not knowing whether Madison Avenue is a block, a mile, or ten miles away.

We could find the answer by asking our guide. But Alexei, gracious and accommodating as he was, worked for the government and, in all likelihood, reported to the police. If we asked him for a specific address, we registered the fact that we were or wanted to be in touch with a particular person in Russia and, quite possibly, jeopardized his safety.

Despite our discretion, I realize today that our mere presence may have hurt the kindly people who were so hospitable to us. The quiet-spoken, sixty-year-old dentist, Dr. Gedalia Pechersky, who served as head of the Leningrad Congregation, is now languishing in a Soviet prison. He faces a 12-year sentence on the charge of making contacts with foreign powers. Thinking back over the many hours we spent together, I cannot recall a single word or gesture on the part of our gracious host that in any way reflected criticism of his government.

Is there freedom of religion in Russia? To answer this we must distinguish between freedom of religion and freedom of worship. In some measure, Jews are free to pray. Mr. Mikoyan, during a conference with leaders of the American Jewish Committee in New York, blithely spoke of religious liberty; yet even freedom of worship is limited. A Russian Jew may enter a synagogue to pray—if he knows the date of a Holy Day. He cannot find this information in *Pravda*. His synagogue publishes no bulletin, as does the Russian Orthodox Church, nor does it issue a religious calendar. Even in matters of worship, the people of this land walk in darkness.

How does one obtain paper and a press to publish information? Every synagogue activity is channeled through the office of the Council of Cults. Neither a new electric bulb, nor a quart of paint, nor a pane of glass for a broken window can be purchased without permission of this Council, which maintains rigid control over the most trivial activity of the congregation.

For the traditional Jew to pray without Hebrew is like trying to sing without breathing. Yet it is forbidden to teach Hebrew to a person under eighteen.

I met an elderly worshiper who came to pray at six o'clock in the morning every day of the week, but felt forced, for fear of reprisal, to work on the Day of Atonement. Thus, the words of reassurance by Messrs. Mikoyan, Koslov, and Khrushchev have a tragically hollow sound.

Granted that there is some freedom to worship, freedom

of religion, as we understand it, is unknown in the land of the Soviets. We asked a government official: "May the congregation remain after services to learn the Hebrew of the prayer book?" He replied: "That would be transforming a house of worship into a school."

The Kafka-like feeling of unreality was with us during our entire stay. After a while, we began to wonder if our senses were playing tricks. We asked the Chief Rabbi if we could send him prayer books, prayer shawls, and other ceremonial objects which we found in such short supply. (Some old people pleaded with us to give them prayer shawls so they could be buried according to tradition.) The rabbi answered: "Of course—if the secretary of the Council of Cults gives his approval." In the latter's office, the Soviet official said: "Of course, you can send them—if the rabbi tells you he needs them." Then he wryly added: "The trouble with your rabbis is that they're afraid to ask." We wondered what happened to the last rabbi who had the temerity to do so.

We engaged in a battle of wits with Alexei, our guide, who humorlessly led us from art galleries to museums to agricultural exhibitions, while we kept prodding him to bring us closer to his people. One of the rabbis devised a scheme: "Alexei, get me a chess game." A few hours tête-à-tête with an individual Russian, he thought, might be more revealing than a tour of the Kremlin. Alexei kept postponing his answer—he never said "no." On the fifth day in Moscow, my colleague took our guide by the shoulders and dramatically informed him that one more day without chess might have dangerous consequences for his nervous system.

"Don't worry, Rabbi, I'll arrange it today."

That afternoon he walked into the hotel dining room wearing half a smile. "I've found a chess player for you."

It was another American tourist who had asked his guide for a game.

The problem of penetrating the second, or inner, curtain is almost insuperable. For it is completely invisible—a psychological pall which prompts the person sitting next to you

in your pew, before worship begins, to move to the other
side of the synagogue. The Chief Rabbi, sitting informally
around the supper table, speaks of the glories of Soviet religious liberty, while two aides sitting on either side of him
take notes of our conversation. Is he talking to us, we wonder,
or for the record?

Those of us who want to help our coreligionists are constantly faced with this dilemma. How can we establish the
truth of information given us when, to prove its validity, we
must expose our informants to reprisal? Even as we call attention to the abysmal gap between Soviet pretensions and
the facts as we saw and heard them, we are aware that the
very people we are trying to help are thereby placed in
further jeopardy.

Visitors to the Soviet Union return with totally conflicting
reports about Jewish life. The ordinary tourist, who generally
manages only a casual acquaintance with a few Russian
Jews indifferent to the survival of Judaism, may come away
with the impression that many of his coreligionists are happily
integrated into the social, economic, and political life of the
country. Almost lyrical, too, are the statements of Soviet
writers and military leaders visiting in the West, who cite
their own Jewish background as unchallengeable proof that
anti-Semitism is unthinkable under Khrushchev. When we
asked a Moscow official why Jews are not granted the privilege
of emigration, he replied with a combination of blandness and
asperity: "Why, who would want to leave our country?"

On the other hand, those of us who journeyed to Russia,
committed to a belief in the perpetuation of Judaism, who
searched out those who shared our convictions, found the
atmosphere dark with foreboding. On the evening of July 4,
we attended services near midnight—the sun does not set
till after 11 P.M.—and we told some of the worshipers about
our meeting with Khrushchev, Molotov, Malenkov, and Bulganin. They had been most amiable—especially Molotov and
Bulganin—and had asked us, in good chamber-of-commerce
fashion, how we were enjoying our visit. (We did not tell

them that a diplomat from one of the Scandinavian countries predicted two or three of the gentlemen would soon fall from favor.)

"Why are you so fearful?" we asked our fellow worshipers. "Hasn't Stalin's reign of terror come to an end?"

They responded wearily—those who would speak—in the soft shadows as we walked from the synagogue. Things were better for the moment, but who knew how long the new spirit would continue?

These Jews distinguished between religious observances that were of permanent duration, and those which were ephemeral. To attend worship was fairly safe, although one still had to guard one's tongue in the presence of "kookers" (spies). It was assumed that no one reported who attended worship and who did not. But to be married in the faith, or to have their children circumcised, these were deeds of record and might some day, in a renewed period of repression, rise to haunt them.

Do we then write off the three million Jews in the Soviet orbit?

I say, no. We must not close the book of Russian Jewish history—a book that spans so many centuries of glory and travail.

On the day before we left New York for the trip to Soviet Russia, four people came to my office—two brothers and two sisters from Newark, New Jersey. They had read about our forthcoming tour and begged me to look up their niece. "Our brother is dead. We last heard from him in 1948, but she must still be alive."

In Leningrad, shortly before we left for home, I handed a slip of paper to the man sitting next to me at morning worship and asked him to inform the resident at the address listed on that sheet that an American rabbi would like to see her at the Europa Hotel.

While we were at dinner that evening, an old man shuffled up to us, and mumbled: "Is there an American rabbi looking for me?"

I took him aside. Was he the brother for whom the New Jersey family had been reciting the *Kaddish* (memorial prayer), these past eight years?

"Who are you?" He studied me with some suspicion. I took out a post-card picture, taken forty years ago: three brothers and two sisters! A flood of tears fell on the portrait of himself as a young man.

Two days later, I made an excited call from Idlewild Airport to New Jersey: "I saw Aaron, your brother—alive. You can stop saying *Kaddish* now!"

I feel the same way about all our coreligionists in the Soviet Union. We must not mourn their passing as Jews prematurely. Jewish history is full of fascinating quirks. There have been so many moments when all seemed lost, yet the spark of life was always rekindled.

Ancient scholars never bothered to seek explanations for these miracles. It was the hand of God—a most reasonable interpretation.

How else explain the strange impulse of the Kremlin, which apparently seeks the complete extirpation of Jewish loyalties, the total uprooting of all Jewish religious traditions, and yet has promulgated a law which ensures the perpetuation of Jewish consciousness?

The Soviet nationality law, which harks back to Lenin's day, officially regards every native of the Ukraine, a Ukrainian; every person born in Uzbekistan, an Uzbek; and every Jew born anywhere from the Baltic to the Pacific, an *Ivreski*—a Jew. Carrying the label on his identification card, the Jewish citizen of the Soviet Union sees it whenever he registers at a hotel or buys a railway ticket. He copies it on his questionnaire when he applies for college or enters the army. What an irony that a government bent on blotting out Jewish life has made absolutely certain that Russian Jews retain their identity.

Can Soviet Jewry be saved? I would say that even the Almighty needs some assistance. Unless the Free World continues to insist that the Soviet Union, as a member of the

United Nations, observe basic human rights, including such rights as emigration, free association, and the free exercise of religious conscience, the prospects are rather dim. But if the pressure of the Free World's conscience is maintained, there is still hope. A Christian leader once observed to me that the will of the Kremlin could not be broken—but it might nevertheless be bent a little.

Our plane carried us back to America exactly fifty years after my father arrived as an immigrant on Ellis Island. Soon after we returned, since I am very much a sentimentalist, I took my sons, David, then eight, and Jonathan, five, for a ride on the Staten Island ferry. As we left the Battery pier, I told the boys: "Today is a very important day in American history. This morning President Eisenhower signed a bill changing the name of the island we're about to see from Bedloe Island to Liberty Island. Just think. Fifty years from now, you'll be able to tell your children and grandchildren: 'I saw Liberty Island the day it got its name'!"

As our boat passed almost in the shadow of the Lady of Liberty, I looked down to watch the impression she made on the youngsters. This was the first time they had seen the statue. As she came into view, the five-year-old snapped to attention, in salute.

"Jonathan, what are you doing?"

"Daddy, isn't it exactly like the 'Star-Spangled Banner'?"

"Yes, Jonathan," I said. And I thought to myself, "You are the son of a father who has just come back from darkness to light, and the grandson of a man who caught the boat which so many others missed. It is certainly proper for you to salute liberty."

# Song of India

IN THE SUMMER OF 1958 I visited the smallest center of Jewish life in any major city of the free world—New Delhi, India. It is an unusual community in many respects. Not a single Jewish family is engaged in business, commerce, or industry. A large percentage are government officials, among them a deputy secretary in the Ministry of Finance, a judge-advocate in the Indian Navy, and a senior architect who designs embassies. One congregant runs a locomotive for the Indian National Railways. And my host at a Sunday afternoon reception tended in my honor was Mr. B. B. Benjamin, who, in addition to his duties as under-secretary in the Ministry of Irrigation and Power, is president of the congregation and cantor of the synagogue. Indian Jewry can boast of an eighteen-century span without discrimination or persecution.

It was warm on that July afternoon, but not uncomfortably so for the subtropics, and the sari-gowned ladies used their fans sparingly as they listened to the program.

First, the children of the religious school, indistinguishable in appearance from any New Delhi youngster, sang with much gusto "Heveinu Sholom Aleichem." It was a mixture of Israeli and Hindu modes. Then the president-cantor explained that he would like the guest rabbi to hear a few of the local synagogue melodies. He proceeded to chant several Sephardic tunes, supposedly taken from Italian Jewish liturgy, but unlike anything I had heard at services in Rome or Venice.

Finally, Mr. Benjamin implored me to share with them some American synagogue melodies. For the first time in my life I sang in public. To compound the felony, the president placed a microphone in my hand, motioned toward a tape recorder, and announced that my renditions would be preserved for posterity!

My contribution to the occasion was the Sabbath evening hymn "Sholom Aleichem," the most universal melody in American synagogue life, familiar to Orthodox, Conservative, and Reform congregations alike. Looking around, as I sang, at the youngsters clustered at my feet, and the smiling ladies in their colorful saris, I asked myself which was the greater incongruity: the microphone and the tape recorder in this ageless land of India—or the visiting rabbi singing without benefit of vocal talent.

When I had rendered the closing notes of my song, Mr. Benjamin, his white teeth glistening in a broad grin that lit up his dark-skinned countenance, clasped my hands enthusiastically: "That's wonderful, Rabbi. And that melody! A real Indian melody!"

I hesitated to tell him that the version I had chanted, though dotted with traditional East European tunes, had been composed forty years earlier by Rabbi Israel Goldfarb in Brooklyn, New York.

A more recent visitor to the Indian capital reported to me a short time ago that when he attended worship at the same synagogue, the children's choir sang, to his amazement, the familiar Sabbath evening song, "Sholom Aleichem."

# A Peculiar People

ON A VISIT TO MONTREAL a few years ago, I developed a painful sore throat. The doctor I consulted suggested that the use of steam might help relieve the congestion.

Early the next morning the cousin with whom I was staying took me into her kitchen and introduced me to her Japanese housekeeper, a young woman recently arrived from the Orient. Obligingly she boiled up a kettle of water and furnished me with a Turkish towel, and for the next half-hour I sat next to the stove, my hands shaping the towel into a little tent over my head.

On my next visit to my cousin's home, some months later, the Japanese housekeeper seemed a bit puzzled about something. We asked what it was that was troubling her.

"When is the rabbi going to say his prayers?" she inquired. "I can fix up the kettle in a minute." Since I had neglected to tell her of my sore throat, she had drawn her own inferences about my strange behavior in the kitchen.

I can well imagine her returning to Japan and giving a lecture to the Women's Club of Osaka:

"The Jews in America have many strange customs. When they awake in the morning, they place themselves in front of a kettle of steaming water, place a large towel over their heads, and in complete mystic silence commune for over thirty minutes with their God."

I wonder how much of our anthropological lore about tribal customs among the primitives is based on similar evidence.

And in our own environs, how much do we really know about another man's faith?

# Do Women Count?

WHEN I WAS sixteen I spent a great deal of time in the home of Toronto's senior rabbi, Jacob Gordon. Rabbi Gordon was a thorough traditionalist, but modern and practical in many ways. He would break off from Talmudic studies, for example, and send his son and me out to the tennis courts for a game or two. "A sound body, like a clear mind, are both gifts from God," he would tell us.

Frequently the rabbi asked me to assist him when a wedding party came to his study. Among other duties I had to fill in the necessary documents and guide his hand to the line where he affixed his signature, for Rabbi Gordon was sightless. Since traditional Jewish law requires the presence of a *minyan*, a quorum of ten males, for a marriage ceremony, I often had to scour the neighborhood for a few additional witnesses.

On one occasion the bride grew restless waiting for the quorum to be completed. Somewhat resentful over the implied slur at her sex, she asked plaintively:

"Why don't you count women in a quorum?"

The rabbi smiled indulgently.

"My dear young bride," he explained, "we don't count women in a *minyan* because all women are angels. And you just can't count angels in a quorum."

The impatient bride relaxed. It seemed a logical enough explanation.

# Rugged Individualism

To the unpracticed ear of a visitor to Orthodox Jewish services, the worshipers may seem to be praying more or less in unison. But a latecomer begins with the opening prayers, and may never catch up with the rest of the congregation. American Orthodoxy tends toward conformity and uniformity, but the accent on individualism persists. When I was a chaplain at Fort Dix, I would notice occasionally, in the middle of an impassioned sermon, that one of the GIs would rise unconcernedly to recite his devotions. It did not occur to him that his "going it alone" was disconcerting to the chaplain. He was communing with God.

When I visited the Soviet Union, I wondered what had happened to Jewish individualism in a state that exacted unquestioning conformity. My answer came when I attended services in Moscow, and later in Leningrad. Not only did each worshiper proceed at his own pace, but when the Torah service began at the spacious Leningrad Synagogue, three scrolls of the Law were removed, and three readers intoned the Biblical words separately, so that twenty-one members might be honored by being called to the Torah instead of the usual seven.

Other Russians, however, in the stores, at railway terminals, and in government offices all seemed docile and submissive to authority. Less than a block away from the synagogue, a news vendor stood in the rain, getting ready to sell *Pravda* and other papers. A score of people waited uncomplainingly in a queue while he chatted with a friend. A French tourist muttered to me: "Before we Parisians got soaked in the rain, we'd give that man a piece of our minds."

175

Following Sabbath morning worship, our hosts entertained us at a luncheon, which began with the sanctification over wine (*Kiddush*) and the ceremonial washing of hands. Then the president of the congregation, Dr. Pechersky, rose to greet us. Several of the congregants entered during his remarks. Ignoring their president, they proceeded to chant the wine blessing, turned on the water at the sink, and praised the Lord with unrestraint: "Praised art Thou . . . Who hast enjoined upon us the commandment of washing of the hands."

I could now appreciate the extent of the Soviet problem with the Jews. How can that state digest a people who have thrived on individualism for the past 2,000 years—a people whose folklore includes such gems as "Two Jews—three opinions," and "The only thing on which two Jews will agree is what a third should give to charity." Even in Israel the Jews are not content with two or three political parties, but insist on modeling themselves after the highly individualistic French with twice the number of France's political parties.

Judaism is incompatible with communism not only for ideological reasons, but for temperamental ones as well. That's why when we Americans tried to follow the words of the Russian synagogue president with one ear, while a few of his congregants were "operating on another network" at the same time, we were only momentarily annoyed.

Nebuchadnezzar of ancient Babylon had his trouble with his "conquered" Hebrews; the Emperor Trajan never could digest his Jews in a Roman brew. What chance, then, does Khrushchev have?

# Japanese Journey

A FEW YEARS AGO a flurry of excitement passed through Jewish communities throughout the world over newspaper reports that four thousand Japanese had been converted to Judaism. The dateline of the story was Jerusalem, not Tokyo, and later it was revealed that some four thousand Jews from Manchuria, whose origins were Russian and Ukrainian, had spent the war years in Japan, and were now settled in Israel. But the rumor persists that large numbers of Japanese, tired of Shintoism, are turning to the faith of Moses.

When I attended services at the Tokyo Jewish Center during my visit to the Orient, I looked carefully among the worshipers to see if there were Orientals among them. There were three of them. One, a young man, was an authentic convert. He had changed his name, in accord with traditional practice, from Shiguru to Shlomo, and was about to depart with his wife and two children for an Israeli kibbutz. Though he had embraced our ancestral faith, he seemed far more interested in the people of Israel than its religious doctrines.

The second was a middle-aged man, Professor Kobayashi of Waseda University, about whom much has been written. We spent many hours together in subsequent days, and I discovered that the history professor was not a convert. He loved synagogue music, was enamored of Jewish folkways. He had read every word of the classic Jewish historian Graetz, and had been attending synagogue worship every Sabbath for many years. But withal, he had no intention of becoming a Jew. I mused that the professor had many more earmarks of Judaism than most believers, though he could not be called a Jew.

Dr. Kobayashi's interest was in the Jews, not in Judaism, and he is the expert on European Jewish history at Japan's largest university. Was it true, I asked him, that his people were attracted to Judaism? Professor Kobayashi told me a remarkable story. During World War II, their Nazi allies had pleaded with the Japanese to turn over the Jewish refugees for concentration-camp treatment, but like the Italians, they refused to do so. As a compromise, the Jews were moved out of Tokyo for security reasons—a happy event, for they were spared the misery of Allied bombings, and the mountain detention place was so pleasant that the Jews now living in Tokyo use it as a kind of Catskill summer retreat.

Several propaganda writers, following the Nazi line, wrote anti-Jewish pamphlets, warning the Japanese against sinister Jewish control. Their words fell on deaf ears, however, for the tiny Jewish community was virtually invisible.

"In the last year of the war," declared Professor Kobayashi, "we were totally unprepared for defeat. We had been told that Chicago and Los Angeles were obliterated and that we had conquered all the Pacific. When our leaders sued for peace, many Japanese were confounded. The propaganda writers, who had been preaching the gospel of Jewish domination of the Allies, apparently believed what they were writing; several of them are now publishing pro-Jewish books and pamphlets, on the theory that it is wise to be on your side."

Recently the Tokyo historian attended worship in my temple on his way to Cincinnati, where he did further research in Jewish studies.

The third Oriental worshiper in the Tokyo synagogue was a nineteen-year-old girl, Uchida. I think that the word "winsome" was coined to describe this type of Japanese young woman, soft spoken with an engaging smile and a captivating grace of manners. Born of Buddhist parents, Uchida had become an Episcopalian, to the chagrin of her parents, at the age of fourteen, and was employed at a Catholic college.

"I've been coming to this synagogue regularly for the past year. I didn't know a thing about your religion, but here in

Tokyo I've met some half a dozen Jewish people from America, and a Jewish chaplain. There must be something about Judaism that makes people nice, because every Jew I've met is nice." She hesitated a moment. "I guess there are some who are not so nice, too, but I haven't met any."

That seems as good a reason as any to come to a synagogue.

The only other Japanese Jews I know are the Okamotos, a young couple who also came to Judaism of their own initiative, attracted by ideals which appealed to them. In the Okamoto home in Cincinnati, where the husband is studying at Hebrew Union College, we sat on the floor around a low table, enjoying our sukiyaki dinner. Our hostess, Kyoko, wore a kimono and sash and, after the meal, distributed Hebrew prayer books so everyone could join in the grace. It was quite a sight: the young man with almond-shaped eyes wearing a skullcap and swaying in Hasidic fashion as he intoned: "Praised art Thou, O Lord our God, Who dost feed us all . . ."

Kyoko sang all the melodies in a bell-like voice, the Hebrew words falling from her lips without accent. Her twenty-month-old baby, Shemaiah, was named for an ancient Talmudic rabbi who lived in the time of Herod in another part of Asia, ten thousand miles distant from their native land. She was proud of the way her husband took care of the baby, unlike the men back home. "He's a good *Jewish* father, my Hiroshi."

The newspaper accounts about Japanese converts were slightly exaggerated. There are not four thousand Japanese embracing the religion of Israel; just four. But in the long-range history of Judaism, there may be infinitely more drama in the fact than in the fiction.

# A Seat in Heaven

THE CITY OF SAFED, in Israel, perched high in the hills of Galilee, is an extraordinary town, the seat of Jewish mysticism for over a thousand years. Its fortress heights have been scaled by Roman invaders and by the Crusaders. And through the centuries Jews with a bent toward the mystic have made their pilgrimages to this historic community.

I walked into a book store on Safed's main street operated by a Mr. Luria. The name should have forewarned me that the proprietor was likely to have cabalistic connections, for Rabbi Isaac Luria came from Cairo in the sixteenth century to found a school of mysticism that has made his name revered in Judaism.

After making my purchase, I chatted with the owner. Did I know, he asked, that when the Messiah came, all the children of Israel, living and resurrected, would be gathered into Jerusalem? I told him that I had read about it, but he detected a hint of skepticism in my voice.

"Of course, when that day comes," he assured me with fervor in his voice, "there will not be seats for everyone. People like yourself will have to stand. There will be seats enough only for the descendants of the House of David. Naturally, the Lurias, who trace their ancestry back to the sainted Rabbi Isaac, and before him to the greatest of all Jewish scholars, Rashi (of the eleventh century), and through them to the kings of Judea—all of us will be comfortably seated in Jerusalem." He looked at me, genuinely regretful that I would not qualify.

180

One Saturday afternoon a few of us walked up several hundred steps on the slopes of Safed. As we stopped to catch our breath, a bright old lady asked us if we were going to the synagogue.

"I'll be glad to show you the way. I'm going to a ladies' Bible class conducted by the rabbi's widow."

Our guide, sprightly despite her ninety-five years, did not bother to conserve her breath as we did.

"I'm a great-great-grandmother. I'm a midwife and some of my babies are now great-grandmothers. I suppose you know that, according to our tradition, once you become a great-grandparent, you are guaranteed a place in Heaven."

We expressed delight at her good fortune.

She frowned momentarily. "It's a *zchus* all right (a blessed achievement). The only trouble is, now that I'm guaranteed a heavenly seat, I'm too old to sin!"

# A Child's-Eye View

I HAD JUST COMPLETED A TRIP around the world. David, my ten-year-old son, and Jonathan, seven, regard flying as rather routine, but they were obviously relieved when their father completed the global tour without incident. I overheard their whispered conversation in another room:

"Let's buy Daddy a coming-home present. How much do you have?"

Their combined resources totaled thirty-five cents.

"That's enough for a paperback book. What kind do you think Daddy would like?"

"Maybe we ought to get him something religious."

"That's right. He's a rabbi."

"D'you think we can get that kind of book for thirty-five cents?"

A half-hour later the two appeared, breathlessly, package in hand.

I unwrapped the "surprise" gift. On the bright cover of the book was a drawing of a half-clad girl. The title: *God's Little Acre*.

Jonathan's mind has always tended toward the speculative.

"Is it true," he asked us at the age of four, "that we come from seeds?"

"Yes, Jonathan."

"Does that mean that you came from a seed? And David? And Ruthie?"

"Certainly. Everybody."

A light dawned on his face.

"Now I know why they call people 'human beans.'"

*Remaking Our World*

# In the Image of Man

WE AMERICANS have an infinite capacity for wearing our hearts on our sleeves and at the same time feeling foolish about our romanticism. We laugh at the superficiality of Mother's Day observances, and each year we buy more cards and send Mom more flowers and telegrams. And now that we've gotten to the point where jokes about mother are hardly funny any more, brotherhood has replaced motherhood as the butt of those who regard sentiment with suspicion.

Of course we are rightfully suspicious of many pious pronouncements about good will and religious togetherness. Even as we join in singing "The More We Get Together," the cynic within us keeps nudging: "Some people—the more you know them, the better you like them; but others, the more you know them, the *less* you can stand them!"

That's why, I must confess, I've always had some reservations about the annual celebration of Brotherhood Day—though in all fairness to its sponsors, the National Conference of Christians and Jews, we've all come a long way from the so-called era of good will when trifaith teams traveled through the land chorusing: "I love you, and you love me—we're all one happy family!"

Happily, we've outgrown many of the primitive notions we once entertained about brotherhood. Certainly we have developed beyond an earlier belief in the magic of words. There was a time, two decades ago, when some of us thought that all we really had to do was to repeat constantly such words as tolerance and good will and, through some process of osmosis, mutual understanding would come to us. Today

185

we realize that neither words nor intentions are contagious—
but actions are.

A second sign of maturity in intergroup understanding is
seen in the more sophisticated, relaxed attitudes of minority
groups. Back in the 1930s, many Jews felt it absolutely in-
cumbent upon them to defend their good name against every
libel or canard. If some bigot in Topeka, Kansas, spread the
nasty rumor that all Jews were rich bankers, we dispatched a
team of experts to assure the fair-minded citizens of Kansas
that the world was full of miserably poor Jews. Books and
pamphlets were published to demonstrate "The Jewish Contribution to Civilization" or to document our patriotism to the
Colonies, to the Republic, to the North—and to the South. In
order to prove that Jews did not have horns, we were determined to convince our Christian neighbors that we all had
wings. "Look at Albert Einstein; look at Judge Louis D.
Brandeis; remember Chaim Weizmann who helped Lloyd
George win the First World War."

The trouble is, this technique won few converts. Bigots,
almost by definition, possess a soaring imagination. For every
charge laid to rest, another score rose up to plague us. Many
years ago, my wife and I, aboard an ocean liner bound for
Europe, played bridge with a Mr. and Mrs. S., of Fort Wayne,
Indiana. Examining my hand, I opened the bidding with "one
no-trump."

"It's a strange thing," commented Mrs. S. "Jews always
bid no-trump."

"That's an interesting observation," said my wife, in a
matter-of-fact tone. "We happen to be Jewish."

Mrs. S. turned red; her husband, a pale yellow. But the
lady from Indiana quickly recovered: "They usually bid no-
trump—but they *always* make it!"

Israel had been redeemed!

A mature approach to interfaith understanding perceives
clearly that wholesome relationships are based on seeing our
neighbors as human beings who share our own frailties and

blemishes. When I read Hartzell Spence's portrayal of life among the Methodists in his delightful *One Foot in Heaven* I didn't become anti-Methodist because he depicted some of the pettiness among members of a Methodist congregation. "Methodists are just as bad—or as good—as Jews," I thought to myself. Man may be born in the image of God, but we might as well make peace with the fact that he is also born in the image of man.

Some time ago I told an interfaith audience in Dallas about a Passover Seder service I once conducted in Sing Sing prison. That was one of the most rewarding experiences of my life. What a place to celebrate the Feast of Liberation! The hall was filled with happy prisoners munching matzos. And when that "congregation" sang "Let My People Go," they really meant it!

I told my Dallas listeners that we were much less self-conscious, as members of a minority, about telling such stories to Christians. "A decade ago I would have hesitated to mention to Protestants and Catholics that I found Jews in Sing Sing. Or I would have tried to lessen the sting by quoting statistics to prove that Jewish prisoners are fewer than the ratio of Jews in the population."

After my address, a man approached me. "My name is O'Brien," he said smilingly. "It was good to hear you talk about the Jews in Sing Sing. All my life I thought only Catholics got there."

Many influences have contributed to the more relaxed atmosphere in American interreligious relations. Of no small importance is the general economic picture. A great deal of intolerance has its genesis in economic want. Hitler's maniacal pleading might well have fallen on deaf ears if more of his audiences were regularly employed.

Unquestionably the experiences of many Americans in military life have played a part in their change of attitudes. In the past twenty-five years, selective service has exposed many millions of young men for the first time to fellow Americans of differing religious traditions. GIs—even those who have never seen a foxhole—share their lives in an intimate and deeply meaningful way.

During World War II, I was transferred from Italy to France on the eve of the High Holy Days. When I arrived at my destination I discovered that we had no prayer books for Rosh Hashanah. My senior chaplain, Father Patrick Fay, volunteered to hitch a plane ride from Marseille to Rome, where I knew there was an ample supply; and a few hours before we ushered in the New Year, Father Fay arrived with the books. Over seven thousand Catholic, Protestant, and Jewish clergymen wore the uniform of our military establishment during World War II. The uniform did not breed uniformity, but it certainly gave us enduring fraternity.

In the battle against bias, we have acquired a powerful ally during the postwar years in the psychological sciences. Dynamic psychology has provided profound new insights into the mechanics of prejudice. We have developed a new vocabulary, especially in understanding the nature of the so-called authoritarian personality. True, it may be only a limited comfort to a victim of prejudice to know that the man who hates him is a hostile human being, full of hatred even for himself. But it does mean that we who are scapegoats can stop asking ourselves the tormenting question, "What's wrong with *us*?" And, as author Selma Hirsh points out in *The Fears Men Live By:* "We may not be able to argue the highly prejudiced out of his feelings, but we can control some of his actions that spring from them."

It's depressing to realize that bigotry will probably be with us as long as some people grow up in homes without love, broken homes, disturbed homes, homes in which there is no parental understanding or harmony. Nevertheless, it is great progress to recognize that the struggle for intergroup amity is bound up with America's colossal task of achieving emotional health for its citizens.

There is a new realism, too, in our expectations with respect to the Church and the Synagogue as supporting weapons in the fight for brotherhood. Ironically, though religion has its *raison d'être* in the principle of love, many men and women wear its banner to project their own hostilities. Bonaro Overstreet in her insightful essay, "The Unloving Personality and the Religion of Love," points out that "the church attracts to itself in conspicuous numbers certain types of unfulfilled, unloving personalities." And these people do not always remain on the fringe of its life. Indeed, Dr. Overstreet declares, "The internal policy of a church dedicated to the religion of love is often largely determined by those who are basically unloving."

I do not mean to suggest with these words that our religious institutions are the chief sources for bias, but rather that they are not automatically instruments for promoting brotherhood. Perhaps the ideal church or synagogue should insist not only on a creedal test for membership but on a "love test" as well. All who fail would be placed on probation until they give evidence of an emotional as well as a spiritual capacity to love their neighbor.

It seems to me that a mature approach to interfaith co-operation also suggests these additional guiding principles:

First, intergroup peace must never be achieved through a compromise of our basic convictions. A Roman Catholic, whose own interpretation of our Constitution permits the use of tax funds for church schools, must not be required to relent merely on the grounds of intergroup amity. Nor should anyone expect American Jews to soften their concern about sectarian intrusions into the public schools, for the sake of community peace, precious as that is.

The fundamental ground rules for all Americans include mutual respect and consideration, but there must continue to exist, for Protestants, Catholics, Jews, and humanists alike, the most vigorous competition in the free market place of ideas.

True brotherhood is fashioned not only by what we say to and about one another in public but also by what we say about one another in the intimacy of our own group. To compromise in public is often to drive underground the differences which exist—and which, if hidden by a façade of false amity, can corrode the true bonds of brotherhood.

To have any lasting impact, interfaith co-operation must have truly communal goals. I see little value in all the "dialogues" designed to clear up misunderstandings. True, a session devoted to eliminating common misconceptions has a certain educational value, but it does not change attitudes. It is when the citizens of a community—Protestants, Catholics, Jews, and others—get together to grapple with issues that concern them as human beings—child guidance, the need for adequate recreation facilities, the challenge to civil rights, the threat of atomic extinction, and the like—that real understanding develops. After a while one man looks at the other and sees beyond the sectarian difference a fellow parent, a fellow citizen, above all, a fellow human being, prompted by the same human impulses, the same fears, triumphs, and disappointments.

Such co-operation does not water down primary differences. It distills out of a sense of common destiny and purpose that essential element, love.

For more than twenty years of my professional career, I have labored for interfaith co-operation—and I am filled with optimism. We have tremendous resources at hand. The public schools of the nation have given our churches and synagogues an instructive lesson in community living. Our young people, products of these schools, reject false religious stereotypes, look suspiciously on those who encourage intolerance. The mass media, the entertainment world, the sports world— all have united to encourage respect for differences.

I shall never forget an incident which took place at the University of Iowa, where I was teaching in January, 1942. It was just after Pearl Harbor. A student, Ed Mahoney, came up to my desk wearing a brand-new Army Air Force uniform. He had just received his commission.

"Dr. Kertzer, I'd like you to read this letter from a friend of mine, a Jewish boy stationed at a preflight cadet school in the Southwest."

Ed's hands trembled a little—rather uncharacteristic of this superb athlete who was national intercollegiate swimming champion in his senior year.

His friend wrote that he had been "washed out" of cadet school "because my commander doesn't like our kind."

"Do you think that's possible, Rabbi?" asked Ed.

I suggested that it probably was not true. Sometimes, I explained, we see prejudice when it really isn't there.

"I'll tell you, Dr. Kertzer, I'm willing to fight for an America that gives a man a fair break."

"Don't get too worked up," I told him. "I know Jewish boys on the basketball team, who complain to me, when they warm the bench all evening, that the coach gets his orders from the Nazis."

He stared at me for a moment, half believing, half incredulous.

"You know, Rabbi, I'm not only willing to fight—but to die —for our country, provided it gives a man a square deal."

That was the last time I saw Mahoney. Destiny cast me into the European Theatre of Operations while Ed flew a B-29 over Japan. V-J Day came after he had completed well over twenty missions. He was killed when his plane overshot the runway as he was returning to March Field, California.

But to this day, when I think of America, I think of Ed Mahoney, and others like him of all faiths, whose image of America is all tied up with "giving a man a square deal."

# Shadows of War: Does Religion
# Have an Answer?

WILLIAM I. ELLIOTT'S POEM, *A Summer Nightmare, 1961*,
has its setting in Chicago after the Russians have dropped an
H-bomb on the city. The city is reduced to rubble. Huddled
in their bomb shelter, a little family passes the frightening
time away.

Down in the shelter, eight-year-old Becky had her mind on
important battles:

"Who won, Daddy? Did we win?"

"Turn on the portable and see."

"I did but I can't find a station."

A simple question: After it's over, how can we tell who
won? In these few words the poet sums up what Reinhold
Niebuhr calls "the nuclear dilemma." On the one hand, how
far can the Free World permit itself to be blackmailed? And
on the other, how can we call a halt to such blackmail when
the use of atomic weapons are likely to mean the end of the
very values we would be fighting to preserve—our homes, our
loved ones, our free institutions, life itself.

This question is being asked on two different levels. Many
dedicated men in the upper echelons of diplomacy are cross-
ing and recrossing the Atlantic in search of an answer. On the
whole, these are wise men; some, like Dag Hammarskjöld,
are prepared to sacrifice their lives in this pursuit.

Equally concerned, and even more perplexed and frustrated,
is the man in the street. For the most part we feel like helpless
onlookers, even though we know that what is taking place has

a vital bearing on our lives and our future. In a way, we are all in the position of a patient, listening to the doctors debate a course of treatment that may make the difference between doom and salvation.

Walter Lippmann, in a brilliant article entitled "Nuclear Diplomacy," touches on a crucial factor in our dilemma. None of the statesmen who hold the future in their hands, Mr. Lippmann reminds us, has been taught how to conduct diplomacy in a nuclear age. Kennedy, Khrushchev, Adenauer, Macmillan, DeGaulle—all of them have to guess and improvise, experiment and hope.

What a chilling thought that is. Even those whose fingers are on the master switches are without experience to guide them. And the rest of us are like passengers on a jet transport, hurtling through space at ten miles a minute with a pilot whose hands tremble at the controls while he studies a book entitled, *How to Fly the New Jets in Ten Hard Lessons.*

Is it any wonder, then, that our generation is experiencing, as the ancient Greeks once did, a "failure of nerve"?

How do we deal with this issue of war in our time? Does religion have an answer? I would say yes. Indeed, religion has not one but four answers to this crucial question.

The first may seem merely a bit of Pollyanna, but it's not. Religion has the tremendous job of simple reassurance. We must restore in one another a basic faith in mankind. Not a blind faith, which says that no matter what we do we will not blow ourselves up. Let's admit with the ancient Roman poet that "against stupidity, the gods themselves contend in vain." There seems to be no limit to man's foolishness. Yet, religion must keep stressing our confidence that our fellow man is at least as well motivated as we ourselves are. Fundamentally, my deepest quarrel with the right-wing extremists, the John Birch Society people, is that they deny the central thesis of all religion by dividing mankind into devils and saints. What is worse, they characterize as devils all who refuse to accept *their* diagnosis of any problem. Herein lies the virulent danger of the John Birch people—the General

Walkers, the Senator Thurmonds, and their ilk. They are eager to destroy our confidence in our fellow citizens and our leaders. And if we accept the view that those who guide our destinies lack stamina, lack intellectual capacity, and, above all, lack moral integrity, then indeed we are lost.

The first task of religion, then, is to gird up our confidence in ourselves and in our leadership—our conviction being that whatever their political party, those who are in command are acting out of love for mankind, and with all the wisdom they can summon up within our nation.

And this leads me to religion's second task in these challenging days. What do I mean when I say that our leadership wants to harness the collective wisdom of our nation? The truth is that if all our collective wisdom cannot solve our international problems, we must abandon hope. But actually, how much thought, deliberation, and understanding have we brought to bear on the problem of the East-West conflict?

Put yourselves in the place of the men who guide our destinies. What would you do if these life-and-death decisions were in your hands? It seems to me that you would first and foremost seek to learn what your people want. How far are they willing to go? How do they feel about Berlin, about Laos, about the United Nations—about giving up some of their own sovereignty?

Secondly, you would want the most thoughtful, the most informed, the most dedicated people in the nation to help and guide you. How well equipped is our citizenry with the facts from which to make meaningful judgments? *Every road to disaster is lined with road signs marked "ignorance."* Does the average American know, for example, that the bomb Mr. Khrushchev is now boasting about has a force equal to that of the Hiroshima bomb repeated every day for twenty-three years? Does he know some of the simple facts of history . . . that the military power of one protagonist has never deterred another from war? Is he aware, really *aware*, that if we were to listen to the advocates of a preventive war ("do it first and fast") and the Russians heeded the same clamor, total destruction would have to be the inevitable outcome?

Above the entrance to UNESCO headquarters in Paris is an inscription that reads: "Since wars are born in the minds of men, it is in the minds of men that the defenses of peace must be constructed." Only the ignorant repeat the nonsense that you can eradicate communism by physical force. So long as communist doctrine appeals by virtue of its political and economic successes, and often, let it be admitted, by virtue of our own failures, so long will communism exist and flourish. *Indeed, a post-atomic-war world is much more likely to be communist, or fascist, than democratic.*

If Judaism has taught anything to the world, it has given us this: We must equip ourselves with knowledge—knowledge of ourselves, knowledge of the nature of this universe, knowledge, especially, of what we dislike and oppose. Only a barbarian mocks a brain trust. It seems to me that every church in this country, every temple in this country ought to meet the present emergency by establishing centers of information about world problems. We should sponsor study groups; we should distribute some of the fine pamphlets that are available; we should reprint what Mr. Lippmann, the *Manchester Guardian*, and many other thoughtful sources have to offer.

We are not helpless passengers on a plane flying blind. We can help our pilots steer their course—*if* we equip ourselves with the principles of navigation so that we know exactly where we are and how to get where we want to go.

Walter Lippmann wrote these somber and sober words: "Though a nuclear war would be lunacy, it is a possibility because, however irrational it may be to commit suicide, a nation can be provoked and exasperated to a point where its nervous system cannot endure inaction, where only violence can relieve its feelings. . . . *There is a line of intolerable provocation beyond which governments are uncontrollable.* The governments must know where that line is, and they must stay well back of it." (Italics mine.)

That is where you and I, if we are enlightened and inspired by good will, come in. We can provide our national leadership with the kind of knowledgeable support which will make possible both restraint and action.

A third task for religion stems from the second, that is, not only to know, but to speak out fearlessly, unflinchingly, undeterred by the barking of the obscurantists and the hysterical.

We are now witnessing some of the bitterest battles for peace in contemporary history. The United Nations itself, conceived in war and dedicated to the proposition that peace is possible, is threatened with a paralysis that can only be the prelude to extinction. Now, as never before, every decent element in our society must be summoned to its support.

You will hear many shrill calls to remove the UN headquarters from America. Mr. Khrushchev wants it in West Berlin; many thoughtless Americans simply want it out of existence. Let them call us disloyal, tools of a foreign power, weak-minded sentimentalists—but let them not stampede us into silence or inaction. Prophetic men and women are used to the sound of the mocker, the stones of the unthinking.

A young man in Florida was recently denied a scholarship he won and needed because he had the temerity to criticize that evil film of the House Un-American Activities Committee, *Operation Abolition*. The church and the temple will also have to pay, in mob disapproval, for speaking out with moral vigor. But it is a small price in a world that stands on a precipice.

Finally, there is religion's most direct answer of all to the question of war and peace. It is caught in the essential meaning of the word *Sholom*, our traditional word for peace.

Some years ago, I read an autobiographical novel by William Manners, entitled *Father and the Angels*. "Father" in this engrossing story was a rabbi in Zanesville, Ohio. In one scene, the son, a strapping young man, announced to his parents that he had decided to become a professional boxer. The rabbi and his wife were both appalled. The son of a rabbi . . . a boxer! His mother tearfully pleaded with him: "My boy, you'll get hurt." The young man turned to his father. What did he think? The rabbi answered softly: "My son, you may hurt somebody!"

Most of us, when we grow fearful about a possible war, think of nuclear missiles raining down over *our* heads, *our* homes, *our* loved ones. Those good people in Scotland who protest against the American missile base do so in the language of the mother in the story: *We* may be the target. *We* may get hurt.

But the truly religious person thinks also as the rabbi did— of those bombs his own people are making, and of the innocent men, women, and children far away from us, unrelated except for the ties of humanity, whom those bombs would incinerate. How many of us ever say in our hearts: God forbid that my government, my people, should hurt somebody.

Does religion have an answer? I don't think all religions have the answer we seek. If we subscribe to the dogma that man is essentially evil and will seek combat because he loves combat, because "that's human nature," then we must bow to the inevitability of the next and last war.

We Jews believe that man is born both good and bad, filled with self-seeking passions *and* with an infinite capacity for good and the freedom to determine that good.

Our task is not to brood over man's frailties, his temptations, his baser impulses, but rather to harness our God-given minds to devise a formula that will help us survive in a world of permanently conflicting interests and philosophies.

Is world brotherhood an idle dream? No more fantastic than a United States of America was, two hundred years ago.

It's a bigger task in 1962 than in 1776—more complex, more subtle, infinitely more risky. But if we do succeed, mankind is destined to enter, for the first time in its blood-drenched history, a new Garden of Eden of peace and understanding.

Am I whistling in the darkness of the hour? Let me tell you what sustains me. An old Jewish thought that is expressed in the wonderful Yiddish proverb: *Gott schikt die refuah far der krenk*—"God sends us the cure even before he sends the sickness."

I firmly believe that this trial we face in our lifetime—a test in which the stakes are all of human existence—comes at a moment in man's development when he has unlocked so many of God's cosmic mysteries that his spirit stands poised to soar where his intellect has already taken him.

*How then can man fail?*

# There Were Giants in Those Days

IN THE EARLY DAYS OF 1944 I was a transient Army chaplain in Algiers. The hotel to which I was assigned served as an officers' billet. One night, well after midnight, the officer sharing my room turned on the light and began shouting at me in a thick voice:

"Did you see my fountain pen?"

I mumbled that I hadn't, and he teetered about unsteadily, muttering with half a sob and half a hiccup:

"If ever I lay my hands on the so-and-so who stole my pen . . . My dear, dear wife gave it to me . . ."

In a short while he had worked himself into a real lather. Finally, he pulled out his revolver, pointed it at me, and again demanded to know if I had seen his cherished pen. All I could think to do was to slip the sheet over my head and curl up to make the smallest possible target, hoping all the while that if he didn't see me, he would forget I was there.

Somehow, everything I read about our proposed shelter program reminds me of that experience. It seems to me our plans are far more designed to talk ourselves into an illusion of safety than to provide the real thing. For I am convinced that there can be no shelter in a nuclear war, for either side.

What bothers me most about the whole shelter enterprise is the implication that there *is* an alternative to peace. Yet, many of the most thoughtful and knowledgeable among us warn that if ever there is atomic war, civilization as we know it will cease to exist on this earth.

William L. Shirer, the brilliant chronicler of the Nazi holocaust, recently wrote: "The next war will not last long

and none will ever follow it. There will be no conquerors
and no conquests, but only the charred bones of the dead on
an uninhabited planet."

Of course, there are other experts who do see some survivors
in a postnuclear future—though I have failed to discover
anything convincing on which to base this optimism. Let us
assume for the moment that these hopes are warranted and
life will continue. Shall we start to debate how many survivors there will be? According to an estimate by Harrison
Brown and James Real, published by the Center for the
Study of Democratic Institutions, every resident of Los
Angeles County is likely to be incinerated without exception.
Indeed, this would probably be equally true for every large
city, as Albert Chassler points out in his *Neither Run Nor
Hide*: "Rationally," he writes, "were we to make vigorous
efforts to survive a large-scale nuclear war, we would forget
our existing cities, reconcile ourselves to the loss of their
inhabitants."

If this be so, I wonder if I have the right to say to the
residents of Los Angeles or any other city: "Help me to
build a shelter for my family or my community. It will be
comforting to you to realize in those last awful moments
that a fine group of Westchester citizens will be carrying on
the democratic tradition."

Frankly, I haven't the nerve to make such a demand on
people who, the experts tell us, are almost certain to be wiped
out in the first minutes of a nuclear war. There is something
grossly immoral in a program that writes off a huge portion
of the population—and asks it to help foot the bill for the
illusory safety of the rest. Taxation without preservation!

If community shelters, constructed with public funds are
immoral, what about privately built shelters? The ethical
questions involved have been sharply defined. Shall only the
rich survive? Shall we really load our pistols and keep our
neighbors out? Ancient law suggests that if we are ever faced
with the awful choice of preferring our own life over that of
another, we have no right to engage in an act that will de-

prive someone else of life. "Don't take for granted that your
blood is redder than your neighbor's," the rabbis of the Talmud remind us.

What fuzzy thinking it is to pin the hope of the free world
on survivors. What kind of survivors? What kind of society?
Will the wise survive—or the foolish? People capable of running our social and industrial machinery—or the backward
among us? The whole concept of a foreign policy based on
"survivors" is an affront to everything my religion has ever
taught me.

What is more, it seems to me that the entire notion that
there *can* be no survivors—a notion which every human being
unconsciously translates into "*I* can survive"—deflects and
weakens our resolution to search out every avenue of peaceful negotiation and compromise. Shelters will not make possible a world half irradiated and half free, much as we would
like to think they would. The battle for peace is the only
battle from which any portion of mankind can emerge a vic-
tor.

Yet, I have spoken to people who still conceive of war as a
solution to communism. They argue that there are two kinds
of human beings in this world: those who can be appealed
to by reason, and those who are moved only by threat of
force. I once heard a "responsible" civic leader, involved in a
labor dispute, seriously suggest that the problem would best
be solved by "cracking a few skulls." When I asked him if he
ever knew anyone to change his convictions as a result of a
physical beating, he answered: "Rabbi, the only thing that
will knock brains into *that kind* of person is a good blow to
the jaw!"

For thousands of years, wise men have tried to point out
the fallacy in such reasoning. "Not by might nor by power,
but by my spirit," declared Zechariah. And what Zechariah
called a law of God is, in modern terms, nothing less than a
law of life.

But if we win, say the strike-them-first advocates—assuming
still a "clean," limited war in which we are the victors—if we

win, world communism will be discredited, and the seeds of democracy will be planted in China and Russia. And they really dream of an Age of Victory, when a triumphant (and unscathed) America will carry "the word" to the benighted millions in Eastern Europe, Asia, and Africa, all waiting to welcome as saviors the people who poured destruction down upon them! Don't these people read history?

Tiny Palestine, that incredible sliver of land, could not be pacified in the late 1940s by more than 100,000 British soldiers. The combined power of the British Navy, Army, and Air Force failed to persuade the Jews of Palestine to accept the solution offered by the frustrated Britons, and the Mandate power finally threw up its hands.

Half a million French troops tried for more than seven years to do the same thing in Algeria. Can one really imagine a postnuclear operation of conversion to our way of life?

As Dr. Erich Fromm has underscored, we are still applying modes of thought that belong to a dead and buried past, as though they made sense today. The word "subjugate" had meaning for Alexander and Caesar and Napoleon. It even had temporary meaning for Hitler. But, just as the concept of colonialism has been decently interred, so is the notion of an imposed way of life utterly archaic. Whether we like it or not, we have only one response to Nikita Khrushchev's rasping challenge, "Let's pit our way against yours"—and that is to pick up the ideological gauntlet. *The H-bomb has rendered obsolete all weapons but ideas.*

I have written earlier that in my opinion the ancient Hebrew prophets appeared at the wrong juncture in human history—2,500 years too soon. We need a Jeremiah to tell us the ineluctable facts of human relationships. The old prophet-priest of Anathoth would have reminded those who seek peace through renewed atmospheric testing and a non-ending arms race that a posture of force inevitably evokes a posture of counterforce in a spiral which can lead only to mutual annihilation.

Jeremiah—now there was an expert in underground shel-

ters. During the siege of Nebuchadnezzar, the rulers of
Jerusalem had him cast into a dried-out well. Quite possibly
he survived the final assault on the Judean city because of
his entombment. But I can well imagine the old prophet
stopping near one of my neighbors, busy excavating his lovely
garden, and saying to him:

"What you are building is a shelter for your mind. There
may be some comfort in keeping your hands busy when you
are confronted with such cosmic problems as Laos, Viet-Nam,
Katanga, the Berlin Wall, Hungarian suppression, Castro, and
the places and peoples in tomorrow's disturbing headlines.
But don't delude yourself into believing that by putting a
sheet over your head all these problems will disappear.

"Living in the modest little world of Judea, I naturally didn't
have your problems. If anything happened in Laos in my
time, the news would not reach Jerusalem until my grandchildren were my age. But you've got to pay the price of instantaneous communication, supersonic travel; and your vision
of one world compared to my little dreams of unity is like
Mount Sinai compared to an ant hill. You inhabitants of the
twentieth century, whose fingertips, before too long, may
scratch the surface of the moon, indulge in fantasies of moral
grandeur such as we in our age could not conceive. You dream
of peace on *earth—all over the earth.*"

Let's put down our shovels and get to work in a constructive, meaningful way to make that dream come true. Let's
seek a better understanding of the world we live in, and of
the people—all the people—in it. Let's learn more about the
emerging nations of Asia and Africa, so that we will not be
stampeded into hysteria when some of our citizens prate nonsense about our country "losing China and Korea" as though
they were our chips in an international poker game. And let's
spend more time and thought on the men and women we
elect to make the life-and-death decisions for us.

Some of us may be sorry we were born in this century. It's
true that this age demands titans rather than ordinary men
and women. But if we summon from within ourselves all the

resources of mind and heart which the children of God, by virtue of that divine spark within us, possess, then we, the first children of the atomic era, may yet fashion such an enduring society of men that generations not yet born will say of us: There were giants in those days.

# Healing and Thinking:
# Joys of the Mind

SAINTS HAVE NEVER BEEN the object of veneration among Jews. But since we all need some form of adulation, Jews venerate doctors. There are only two pedestals higher than a doctor—the specialist and, in recent years, the medical researcher. The folklore on the subject of Jews and medicine would make a massive library. Under the heading of "my son, the doctor" alone, several bulky tomes could be collected.

One of the major indoor sports of the Jewish community, before the days of film and television, was the endless maternal exchange of filial accomplishments known as *sheppen nachas*. In this setting, a parent reported on the progress of her doctor-son and acquired for herself a shining place in the social constellation.

Jews have had a proclivity for medicine ever since ancient times. The most beloved figure in all of Jewish history was the rabbi-physician Moses Maimonides (1135-1204), a man fantastically learned in the wisdom of the ancient Greeks and, in a matchless way, the greatest authority on Jewish law.

One reason medicine holds such a special place is that Jewish tradition views the human body with infinite respect. The rabbis saw in the Biblical declaration that man was made in the image of God a mandate to treat the body with dignity. That explains the Orthodox objection to cremation of the dead and the requirement that an amputated limb must be buried with a measure of reverence.

Tradition enjoined the Jew to consider the normal, healthy

functioning of this body as a sign of God's grace. Indeed, even the Creator was compared to a physician. A whimsical Talmudic story, nearly 2,000 years old, tells of a patient who went to a doctor with a bad wound. When the doctor said, "Your wound grieves me very much," the patient retorted: "Why should you feel bad? The worse the wound, the bigger your fee." In the same way, says the Talmud, King David suggested to the Almighty: "Why grieve over our sins? The greater they are, the more indebted we are to Thee."

Jewish law specifically states that man has an obligation to stay healthy—for only in good health can he truly worship his Maker. The physician thus became God's assistant in Jewish eyes. Pain was not viewed as a sign of heavenly anger, as Job's friends implied, or a nonexistent phenomenon, as in Christian Science, but a signal to man to adopt corrective measures.

I think a second reason for medicine's popularity among Jews is that it satisfies a thirst for adventure. The Jewish community produced few Magellans or Marco Polos. They generally had little interest in reaching out to the poles, or to the ocean's floor. Physical combat, too, has always been alien to the Judaic spirit. But how exciting the uneven battle against diphtheria which attracted Schick, the war against pneumonia which brought Frankel to isolate the pneumococcus, the seemingly hopeless struggle against polio that fired Jonas Salk, and similar challenges that drew so many others.

It is a challenge always mixed with compassion. In 1936 I visited the early Hadassah Hospital installations in Jerusalem and watched the nurses and doctors hovering over Oriental Jewish youngsters and Arab infants in an out-patient clinic. At that time, the Arabs were boycotting all Jewish enterprises. A daily radio broadcast from the hospital pleaded: "You may shun our stores and factories, but for the sake of your babies, don't boycott our life-giving clinics." It was obvious to the visitor that what animated the researcher in pediatrics and ophthalmology was more than simple scientific curiosity. They wanted desperately to help the babies of the trachoma-plagued Orient—with only one chance in five for normal vision—to see something of God's world.

Of course, medicine has long been a status symbol of Jews —and often a way of escape from persecution.

During many centuries, a physician in the service of the King, the Sultan, or the Pope (even Richard the Lion-Hearted invited Maimonides to join his staff) could rid himself of ghetto disabilities. (If his healing arts failed him, though, the full brunt of anti-Semitism was likely to come down on his head.) Later, in the eighteenth and nineteenth centuries, the Jewish doctor continued to win a greater social acceptance in the gentile world than could most of his coreligionists.

In the final analysis, however, the Jewish passion for medicine cannot be separated from our historic attachment to the life of the intellect. Did Jews flock to the arts, the sciences, the colleges because they had become an urban people, or did they stream into the big cities, long out of bounds for them, because the joys of the mind were available to them there? Even in backward Poland during the 1920s a quarter of all the university students were Jewish.

Intellectualism, or the pursuit of ideas for their own sake, is certainly not unique to any culture. But it is generally a fringe tradition, affecting a tiny segment of any group. In the European Jewish community, it was the basic life-style of the entire people. Most of us think of the vast network of Eastern European *yeshivot* as academies for the training of rabbis, and so they were. But with the exception of a select few, the rabbis in training were not being prepared for the pulpit. Their schooling was nothing more than a prelude to a life of study—abstract, impractical study, with no other purpose or goal than the cultivation of the mind and a knowledge of God's law. Thousands of young men spent their lives in this rarefied realm of abstruse ideas, supported by working wives, or by fellow Jews—often without great means themselves—who regarded it a *mitzvah,* a sacred duty and privilege, to use their own mundane occupation thus to strengthen the work of the Lord.

*Fortune* magazine reported, some years ago, that about half of the young nuclear physicists in the United States are Jewish. It is only a short step, it would seem, from the abstract world of the Talmudic academy to the sheltered tower of the theoretical scientist. Possibly, as ghetto memories recede, and the life-style of Jews becomes indistinguishable from that of their neighbors, the tide of Jewish interest will turn toward the more practical professions—engineering and the applied sciences. The world will be the poorer for it.

One final thought on this matter of the joys of the mind. The ancient Hebrews did not always find the fruits of knowledge tasty to the palate. The very first tale in the Bible, the temptation of Adam and Eve—a story so mystifying that even the commentators find no agreement as to what the Biblical author was trying to say—implied that knowledge is not necessarily a boon to man. Many centuries later, the world-weary author of Ecclesiastes, who saw vanity in all human experience, was particularly troubled on this score. "The more knowledge, the more sorrow," he wrote, in obvious distress of spirit.

Like all generalities, this too contained but a modicum of truth. Certainly knowledge brings us pain: the physician aware of a malignancy within his own body suffers a greater mental anguish than the medical innocent similarly stricken. And those of us who clearly perceive man's potentialities for nobility grieve all the more at the widening chasm between what is and what might have been.

Yet, given a choice between the travail of knowing too much and the serenity of ignorance, Judaism invariably chose the former. Better to walk in the light with a heart tinged with sadness than to journey in the dark with a fool's glee.

# The Art of Being a Friend

In the newspaper accounts of a recent airplane crash, there was repeated mention of the fact that one of the victims was mourned "by his friend, Dwight D. Eisenhower." Such an obituary is unorthodox. While it is customary at the time of death to record the names of surviving relatives, including those whose emotional ties may have been quite tenuous, there is seldom any reference to friends—though often these are the persons most saddened by the passing.

I recall officiating at the funeral of a spinster, in her middle seventies. Before the services I asked her nieces to tell me something about their aunt.

"Aunt Martha was just an old crotchety woman, self-centered, intolerant . . ." This was their image of the deceased.

At the cemetery, I noticed an elderly man at the graveside, his face torn with grief, tears on his cheeks unwonted for the aged. On our way back from the service, I asked him if he were a relative.

"No—*just a friend.* We met in the park, when she was seventy and I was seventy-five. For the past seven years, we've been good friends. Did you notice her face, rabbi? Beautiful. Angelic. You know why? Because she was an angel—sweet-tempered, kind, loving . . . a beautiful face." A week later I learned that that had been his own last day on earth.

Only the ancients seemed concerned about the art of friendship. Aristotle devoted two books to the subject. There were, he wrote, three types of social relationships: the first for mutual benefit, the second for mutual pleasure. Only the third

could truly be called friendship: "That which unites men
who are good and alike in virtue."

Jewish tradition put a high premium on this kind of relationship. The tender story of David and Jonathan and their
undying faithfulness was idealized. Who has not wept over
David's lament over his perished companion:

> Thy beauty, O Israel, upon thy high places is slain!
> How are the mighty fallen!
> Tell it not in Gath . . .
> Ye mountains of Gilboa,
> Let there be no dew nor rain upon you.

In all traditions, love is the classic bond which links friends
together—an altruistic concern for another human being. But
friendship and self-love are not strangers to each other. "In
loving a friend for his own sake, men love what is good for
themselves," wrote Aristotle.

Judaism, which has never taken love lightly, speaks of a
responsibility of friendship which hardly seems congenial to
our modern temper: A good companion has an obligation to
chastise his friend, and to help him erase his failings. "A companion who tells you your faults privately whenever he meets
you is better than a companion who hands you a gold coin
whenever he meets you," wrote Solomon ibn-Gabirol, the
eleventh-century philosopher. What better way to improve
one's character than to listen to moral reproach offered with
affection and patient tact. "Faithful are the wounds of a
friend," says the Bible.

In the Middle Ages, and well into the nineteenth century,
it was the practice of Jews to write "ethical wills." A father
would bequeath to his children not only the earthly possessions he had acquired, but also the moral insights he had
accumulated over the years—the spiritual increment of a lifetime, set down for his children's enrichment. An eighteenth-
century Jew, Alexander Susskind, suggested ways in which
his children could fulfill the Biblical injunction, Love thy
neighbor as thyself: "When I saw that the coat of a friend

was slightly torn," he wrote in his last testament, "I advised him to have it mended. But before offering this counsel, I said to myself: 'My Maker, my Creator! Lo, here I am ready to fulfill the command of Thy holy law, bidding man love his neighbor.' Thereupon I would address my friend, reminding him that a small hole grows into a big one."

Another eighteenth-century father declared in the same vein: "It was oft my way at assemblies to raise my eyes and regard those present from end to end, to see whether in sooth I loved every one of them, whether my acceptance of the duty to love my fellow men was genuine . . . Even if I noticed one who had treated me poorly, then without a moment's delay, I pardoned him and resolved to love him. If my heart forced me to refuse his love, I forced myself to speak to him kindly."

These are certainly lofty standards to impose on the "younger generation." And often, as though the writers of these wills knew how frail human resolution can be, the children were called upon to reread the paternal words weekly for many years after their author had departed.

In the nineteenth century, there was a Jewish movement called *Mussar*—ethical criticism. It was the practice, among the adherents of this movement, to make a periodic pilgrimage to a learned friend, saying to him: "You know me well; you've watched the way I behave and talk and live. Tell me candidly, do you see any faults in me that I might correct?"

The key to this custom, of course, was the climate in which the *mussar* was administered. The friendly critic spoke not in disparagement, not in condescension, and never in malice, but rather with the hope of helping his companion live up to his capabilities. And he who requested and received such chastisement accepted his own imperfections and realized that the remaking of his character depended on this painful self-examination. Blessed was the loving friend kind enough to hold up the mirror!

The practice of ethical criticism has gone out of style. Today there is such an intense allergy to personal censure that even its vocabulary sounds archaic: *chastise, chide, reprove, admonish*. Anyone who ventures to heed the Biblical command and to approach a friend with some friendly criticism, is likely to be met with some acid suggestions for putting his own house in order.

In the cult of popularity which marks our age, the critic is the villain, the kill-joy, the spoilsport who hasn't enough sense to understand that a friend is simply a member of a mutual admiration society. If he raises an eyebrow when his neighbor boasts of outsmarting the Internal Revenue Service or inflating his expense account, he's no friend—by these standards of friendship.

One endless source of amusement is the Hollywood director whose retinue consists solely of "yes men." Or the dictator whose automated staff can say nothing but "Amen." I sometimes wonder what we are laughing at. Are we not all of the same stripe? Woe to those who find a blemish in us!

The road of parental criticism in modern times is also filled with land mines that explode in our faces. Not only are we plagued with the possible traumatic effects of too vigorous admonition, we also are faced with the sad fact that our young people are not at all eager to benefit from our experiences.

"It's an altogether different world, Pop; what can we learn from your mistakes?" The nineteenth-century young man felt himself twenty-five years younger than his parents; our children see us as at least one hundred years behind the times. In this Missile Age, parents have lost their credentials as critics.

Is there any relationship between the steady deterioration of our moral standards—the growing corruption in public and private life, the social disorders that threaten to overwhelm us—and our studied resistance to personal criticism? I cannot help but feel that if we recaptured in our intimate relationships (or are those, too, gone forever?) a receptivity to ethical admonition, in the spirit of ancient *Mussar*, our world might be infinitely more tolerable.

I think our forefathers fashioned a remarkable formula for living by weaving the individual into the fabric of the community in such a way that each member was truly a part of an integrated whole. "We are all responsible one for the other," the Jew heard, from his earliest childhood. In that intimacy no one could resent or resist reproof spoken in love. Today we have lost the intimacy and we shun the reproof—and I am afraid we have also yielded up a great deal of that special love.

# An Ounce of Wit—
# An Ounce of Wisdom

In some ways, the distance between comic and tragic is not very far. From the vantage point of the onlooker, a person who takes himself too seriously—how often the buffoon, the ludicrous character in a drama, assumes such a role —is a never-ending source of amusement. But it is not much of a step from the ludicrous to the dangerous. Adolf Hitler was, of course, the classic illustration of this phenomenon, which Charlie Chaplin's satiric *The Great Dictator* exploited so effectively. It is sometimes hard to know whether to laugh or to cry.

Most of the mischief wrought in this world has been visited upon us by people devoid of humor. The unhappy fact is that some people are incapable of poking fun at themselves, thus lacking one of the most important correctives to character.

We in Judaism believe there is a God-given wit that goes with God-given wisdom. It is no etymological accident that the two words have a common origin. For people with the brightest minds generally have the happy faculty of humor. A towering intellect is frequently combined with a delightful capacity for merriment, waggishness, and even practical jokes. As a seminary student, I often enjoyed the hospitality of Professor Louis Ginzberg. Dr. Ginzberg was unquestionably the outstanding Talmudic scholar of our century. His prodigious erudition was the product of much more than his twelve-hour-a-day study schedule. His mind had the absorptive ca-

pacity of an IBM machine, automatically recording everything his eyes beheld. He never "took attendance" in class,
as the other professors did. But at the end of the year he
could tell each of his students in a class of fifty-five the exact
dates they had been absent from September to May. Professor Ginzberg's works have no match in contemporary Jewish literature.

Guests at his dinner table were treated to profound philosophic observations, mixed with whimsy, outrageous puns,
and the most frivolous kind of banter. His formula for conversation was an ounce of wisdom thoroughly mixed with an
ounce of witticism.

Man is the only animal who laughs, a philosopher once
noted. That's how human beings have been able to retain
their sanity. That sage must have had the Jewish people in
mind. For no other group has so clearly demonstrated the sav-
ing power of humor. I think it's more than a coincidence that
Jews have produced not only a lion's share of Einsteins,
Freuds, Waksmanns, and Salks, but also an extraordinary number of comic writers and actors.

There is a popular folk tale called *The Purim of Poland.*
It tells of a small eighteenth-century Jewish community faced
with the threat of expulsion. Apparently the cruel town leaders were not entirely lacking in compassion, or at least in
sportsmanship, for they offered the Jews one chance to avert
their exile. A debate was arranged in the town square between
a popular Polish scholar and a representative of the Jewish
community. The first one to ask a question his opponent
could not answer would win for his side. If the Pole won, the
Jews would have to leave; if the Jew won, they could remain.

Of course, no Jew wanted the task of spokesman. Neither
the rabbi nor any of the synagogue elders wanted to face the
onus of having brought about their community's expulsion.
Finally Shmerel, the shoemaker, volunteered to debate.

The first question Shmerel asked his learned opponent was:
"What is the meaning of the Hebrew phrase *Eini Yodeah?*"
When his antagonist answered, "I don't know" (which is,

of course, the correct answer), the Jews were declared victorious.

But that isn't the end of the story. The unlettered shoemaker was hailed throughout Poland as a hero, but he was at a loss to understand what all the shouting was about. Asked how he came to think of such an inspired question, he explained:

"It's a strange thing. I'm not much of a student. When I came across the phrase *Eini Yodeah* in the commentary of Rashi, I asked a number of great rabbis and scholars what the words meant. They all gave me the same answer, 'I don't know.' I figured if all the learned men didn't know, perhaps my opponent would not have the answer either."

There is a wry humor in deflating any balloon of egotism, but in this instance, the pinprick is aimed at ourselves. For Jews have long gloried in the role of the intellect in their lives; their heroes have always been scholars; their leaders chosen from those most intellectually endowed. But who rescues his people in their moment of peril? The semiliterate Shmerel.

I find great delight in the paradox of a people who take themselves so seriously as to feel that all mankind will be blessed through them and their teachings, and yet retain the redeeming capacity to laugh at their own self-importance.

# Remaking Our World

WE'VE ALL HEARD about the young man who falls madly in love with a girl, insists he has never met anyone as perfect as she, then marries her with a view to improving her further. I think that's the way most Jews feel about America.

With what passion the early Jewish immigrants sang America's praises: Emma Lazarus toasted the Lady of Liberty in words that every school child since has put to memory. Mary Antin closed her autobiographical paean with the ecstatic apostrophe: "Mine is the whole majestic past—and mine, the shining future." "In America there are even Jewish policemen," wrote another newcomer. "There's no grief of exile over here."

But, like the youth whose rapture is tempered by plans to make his jewel glisten all the brighter, the Jewish newcomer set himself to the task of polishing away any flaws still evident in American life. And his children and theirs, catapulted rapidly into the comfortable middle classes, continued to keep that vision bright. Just as the British Jews have clung to the Labour Party, despite their economic class, so have their American suburban counterparts attached themselves to the New Deal, the Fair Deal, and the New Frontier (a greater proportion of Jews voted for Mr. Kennedy than did Roman Catholics). Jews welcome enthusiastically any plan that suggests room for improvement.

Why do liberalism and Judaism go hand in hand? By all logic, an ancient people, whose unbroken chain of tradition was made possible by conservative, faithful transmission from generation to generation, should incline toward the preservation of the status quo. But Jewish nonconformity goes back to the Biblical prophets—to Nathan, who cried out to the all-powerful King David, "Thou art the man"; to Elijah, who inveighed fearlessly against the injustices of Jezebel and Ahab; to all those other leaders of Israel who risked scorn and abuse to remind their people of their responsibilities to God and man.

Equally strong is the tradition of scholar-heroes. Who were our folk celebrities? While other youngsters heard tales of Richard the Lion-Hearted, the Knights of the Round Table, and the Vikings, the children of the ghetto were told: "Did you ever hear the story about Rabbi Akiba? . . . Have you heard the one about the rabbi of Berditchev?"

This historic attachment to the learned has done much to keep Jews in the camp of the liberals. Tell the most unsophisticated Jewish housewife that a Harvard professor advocates foreign aid, that a University of Chicago scholar has proved segregation weakens the fabric of society, that a University of California authority sees a threat to humanity in nuclear testing, and she is thereby half convinced. The standards of the academic community and its values are almost without question the standards and values of the Jewish community.

Even more persuasive, however, is the argument of compassion. From earliest childhood we are taught that "the children of Israel are the compassionate children of compassionate parents." Whatever brings hurt is an evil; the hurtful is the hateful.

If Congress is discussing aid to underdeveloped countries, a good Jew cannot take a position that would keep food from the hungry. When an injured Negro girl is left unattended at the roadside after an accident, because the ambulance is "for whites only," Jews can only regard it as a sin against God, an intolerable transgression against all laws of pity. Centuries upon centuries of oppressive suffering have made Jews exceedingly sensitive to another's pain—particularly pain induced by man's inhumanity toward his fellow man.

To determine whether a social action, a piece of legislation, or a community custom is moral or immoral, we do not belabor a Biblical verse, as the New Orleans woman tried to do in her dispute with the Archbishop. Ours is a simple, uncomplicated test: Does it hurt anyone?

Of course, part of the explanation for overwhelming Jewish alignment on the side of civil rights and civil liberties relates to the long history of discrimination against Jews. Jews fight for human rights because history has voted them the humans most likely to suffer when those rights are denied. But that is not the only reason. The rallying cry of the prophet Amos: "Let justice well up as the waters, and righteousness like a mighty stream" is too deeply imbedded in the Jewish spirit to permit a parochial concept of justice, or a selfish concern for righteousness.

One ingredient of liberalism is an international outlook. During the Stalinist persecution of Soviet Jewry, the Communists charged that Russian Jews were too "cosmopolitan," meaning they were guilty of an unwarranted concern for people other than Russians. Half a century earlier, czarist bigots had also railed against a mythical international Jewish conspiracy. To the primitive mind, it seems inconceivable that a group of people can love their country deeply, yet stretch their range of concern beyond geographical borders.

Again, the explanation is both theological and sociological. Ask a Jew to contribute to the sufferers of an earthquake in Chile or a plague in Southeast Asia, and he responds automatically. Part of the reaction is pure habit: he has been asked for so many centuries to reach into his pocket for a good cause that, like Pavlov's dog, he has but one response. He may be clannish in seeking out a mate for his children or in selecting certain areas of residence. But there is no provincialism in his giving, as any Red Cross official or cancer-drive chairman will testify. (We used to argue with my mother: "Ma, he'll only use that quarter to buy a drink!" Or, "Ma, how can you invite a man into the house for a sandwich? Who

knows how honest he is?" She had a standard answer: "For a
Jew, it's better to give to twenty undeserving persons than to
skip over one who is deserving.")

But the habit of charity is only part of Jewish willingness
to reach helping hands across the seas. For Jews, perhaps
more literally than any other group of people, recognize their
kinship to men and women the world over. I have a cousin
who grows coffee not far from São Paulo in Brazil. Another
breeds horses on the mountain slopes of Montana. Many of
my relatives are farmers in Israel. A cousin by marriage makes
fine leather bags not far from the Bourse in Paris. My paternal grandfather, after coming to America, decided that there
was not enough piety in the New World, and returned to the
Ukraine.

These family ties are durable. They continue from one generation to another. How can one be an isolationist and a Jew?
Little wonder that the babel of tongues at the United Nations is music to our ears!

Albert Vorspan, Director of Social Action for the Union
of American Hebrew Congregations, commented not long
ago on a public opinion poll which revealed that at the height
of Senator Joseph McCarthy's popularity, 85 per cent of
American Jews expressed a distaste for his views. McCarthy,
Vorspan pointed out, had been very careful to disavow anti-
Semitism. Nevertheless, Jews overwhelmingly rejected his
leadership. "It must have something to do with the special
antenna which history has given them." Appeals to hatred of
the stranger, to distrust of the alien, indeed, to chauvinism of
any kind, violate Jewish instinct.

At the time of this writing, the ultraright groups in America have been cautioning their followers not to fall into what
they call "the booby trap of the conservatives—anti-Semitism." We can appreciate their inevitable feelings of frustration when they discover that all their forswearing of bigotry
will not win Jewish souls. For only those utterly alienated
from the Judaic tradition can shake off three thousand years
of indoctrination that all human beings on the face of the earth

"are brethren, one in spirit and one in fellowship, forever united before Thee." We've been permanently brainwashed with brotherhood.

Analyzing the psychology of extreme-right movements, be they of overt Fascist stripe, or the milder counterparts in America, Great Britain, and France, it is not hard to understand the Jewish allergy. For these extremists invariably react to the pressures around them in a childish, immature fashion. Faced with communist advances, not only in space, but in Latin America, Asia, and Africa as well, their answer is either to pretend these advances don't exist—Titov didn't really orbit the earth at all; Red China isn't really there, because we don't recognize it—or to convince themselves that Soviet progress has only been made possible by result of Western betrayal and conspiracy—a conspiracy that encompasses the Supreme Court, the Secretary of State, and the President of the United States!

But Jews have lived from time immemorial in a world of unresolved problems. Centuries of experience had taught them that life is not made up of neat packages, containing an equal number of questions and answers. A recent widely publicized mental health study in New York City revealed that although a disproportionate number of Jews are affected by some form of neurosis, fewer of them are impaired by their emotional disturbances than are their non-Jewish neighbors. Apparently, we can function fairly well in the face of permanent conflict in our lives.

Challenge may lead to desperation, paralysis, or bitterness —or it may tap our deepest intellectual, moral, and spiritual resources. For many of us the most compelling inducement to creative action is the realization that our sojourn on God's earth is unique and unrepeated. So far as we know, all anyone is assured is a single one-way ticket, no exchanges, no returns. The time limit may not be clearly marked, but our time *is* limited, none the less, and we know it well.

Barbara Ward, in her illuminating book *The Rich Nations and the Poor Nations*, ascribes to Judaeo-Christian influence

that "revolution of rising expectations" which is the insistence on the good life, here and now. Certainly the Jewish
affirmation that our salvation lies in this world alone lends
urgency to the demand that today, not tomorrow, the kingdom of God on earth must be built.

# The Eichmann Trial—
# Dilemma of the Modern Jew

*March 1, 1962*

ON THE DAY Prime Minister Ben-Gurion announced to the world that Karl Adolf Eichmann had been apprehended, I was sitting in my office with an old friend, Father Felix Morlion, of Rome. Father Morlion is a Dominican priest. His reaction to the news was startling, to say the least.

"It just shows you, Rabbi, that my religion is better than yours!"

"How so?" I asked.

"Well, just compare the provisions of our two faiths for taking care of such monsters. The most you can do to the beast is to put him out of his misery.

"A moment's suffering, and then, poof! That's the end. But we Catholics . . . for us he would burn in hell for at least five hundred years!"

I confessed to Father Morlion that there was much merit to his argument. Surely no punishment can measure the crime of the man who personally dispatched to their deaths by torture more than 1,800,000 youngsters under fourteen years of age, close to a million of them infants . . . who deprived humanity, collectively, of over 100,000,000 years of living.

How do you "fittingly" punish such a man? Israel's foreign secretary, Golda Meir, told the United Nations Security Council in June, 1960: "It is not a matter of revenge. In the words of the Hebrew Poet Laureate, Bialik: 'A fitting revenge for

223

Its manufacturer was Mr. Adolf Eichmann. But everyone told me to put that abomination away. We would prefer not to concentrate on horror.

It is for this very reason that I would hope the Israelis do not execute Adolf Eichmann. I would urge Jewry to express its unyielding view against capital punishment . . . even for Eichmann. I would agree with Dean John C. Bennett of the Union Theological Seminary that by *not* killing Eichmann Israel would reaffirm the dignity of the individual, the preciousness of human life.

God knows we have enough indignity in the world. Let us recapture a bit of dignity for ourselves and for all mankind. The compelling moral question is not, shall Eichmann be killed, but shall *I* kill him . . . I, through those who represent and reflect my conscience? No! I, who have not given life, will not take it. That is the only answer for a Jew, whose forebears so eloquently proclaimed, for the first time in history, the sanctity of human existence.

By the measurement of infamy, Karl Adolf Eichmann was a meteoric success—as Torquemada was a success; as Rasputin and Genghis Khan were successes. For their names will be remembered in history when most of us are forgotten. But one success I would not grant Adolf Eichmann. I would not permit him to make me an Eichmann, too. Shall I play the executioner, or delegate anyone else to play that role? No, for I want to look into the mirror the rest of my life and say: There is a man, not a beast!

Some day Adolf Eichmann will die . . . but more important to me is the hope that what he stood for will die in this world; that men will love, not hate; that men will stretch out their hands tenderly and with understanding; that fear, one man's fear of another, will no longer be a part of life.

# Postscript

*June 1, 1962*

I SHED NO TEARS today for Karl Adolf Eichmann.

Mercifully he has been liberated this day from memories of the evils he perpetrated, and from the responsibility for those acts which the world has placed squarely upon his shoulders.

But I weep for my people, that it proffered to the arch-murderer the dignity of going to his death in calm composure, retrieving for a moment that quality of humanity which he lacked in his lifetime.

In the very act of dispatching him to his death and cremating his remains (albeit in consonance with his own Machiavellian request), Israel has denied itself the opportunity to affirm anew the dignity of man.

Justice has been done, implacable justice, with its reminder of reaping the whirlwind. But Israel, being human, fell prey to its own humanity, and missed an important occasion to bear witness to the moral grandeur which was responsible for the nation's birth and constitutes the essential reason for its existence.

# Model People

As one who is totally lacking in manual dexterity, I am constantly fascinated by the skill some children display in assembling model cars, airplanes, and battleships. Studying a chart whose complexity, to me, has a hieroglyphic quality, they patiently fit the minute pieces together into a splendid vehicle or flawlessly working ship.

My own hobby is somewhat different. I collect model people. It's a hobby I would like to recommend, especially to growing boys and girls. The challenge of putting together the intricate parts of personality and character that make up an intriguing human being is at least as exciting and rewarding as the satisfaction of fitting together die-cut pieces of wood and metal. And I have a notion that if young people, whose characters have not yet jelled, engage in this kind of pastime, some of the elements of soul they handle in the process may well enter into their own personality structure.

Along with everyone else involved in the educational enterprise, I keep probing the mystery of character change and growth. What chemical process transmutes a self-centered, frivolous girl, pampered in the atmosphere of elegant suburbia, into the floor-scrubbing wife of a graduate student, content with her tiny two rooms on the third-floor rear? (I often wonder why no crusader has ever tackled the problem of near-campus tenements. Perhaps Ph.D. candidates assume that squalor induces a mood of concentrated study.) What marvelous ingredient mellows a blustering, driving man of thirty into considerate, soft-spoken middle age? Why does tragedy chisel hard lines of bitterness onto some faces, and miraculously mold others with eye lines soft and mouth lines graceful and radiant?

If only we could chart these influences and utilize their components in the educational process. What wouldn't a public-school or religious-school teacher give for such a formula for character training. How does it affect the student to memorize a code of conduct, study the laws of our nation, listen to exalted Biblical passages? It isn't really possible to measure the ethical impact of these influences, yet most of us are convinced that, added one to the other, they do have an effect.

In the same way, I think my suggestion for collecting model people might prove not only fascinating but highly educational as well. A youngster might select two or three men or women whose lives to him suggest nobility of spirit. They need not be the "accepted" heroes and heroines, such as Jefferson, Lincoln, or Edison. Less illustrious names which kindle the particular collector's imagination would constitute equally suitable models for collection.

Once the word gets around to friends and family that the youngster is gathering all the data he can find about his special hero, everyone will be happy to join in the search. Birthdays and other occasions will bring books dealing with the personality selected. Uncle Bernie and Cousin Susan will clip obscure newspaper and magazine items for the scrapbook. Stories and references will be jotted down and passed on, and a serious lifetime research project will be under way.

As an example of what I have in mind, let me describe one of my own favorite personality selections, whom I came upon while teaching at the University of Iowa. Dr. Arthur Steindler, whom I have mentioned earlier in this book, was head of the world-famous Children's Hospital, and was regarded by many doctors as the "Einstein of orthopedic surgery." Here are a few research items I've collected to tell his story.

ITEM 1. My visit to a ward in the University of Iowa's Children's Hospital during "rounds." Dr. Steindler was in his early sixties then and he looked a good deal like Dr. Christian in the movies. I had seen chiefs of hospitals on medical rounds

before, but never one with such a following. Some twenty-
five young residents and internes clustered about Dr. Steindler with worship in their eyes as he commented on a patient's
surgical problems.

There was something unusual, too, about the twenty-five
men in white. Two were Japanese-Americans, brought to the
campus by the doctor despite our Government's wartime
internment of all Japanese; one was Siamese; several others
were Spaniards and Latin Americans. It looked like an international conference of young surgeons. Men came to study
under Steindler from such faraway places as Kakinada, India;
Bidsanulok, Thailand; and Rizal in the Philippines. One, Dr.
Vargas, was the son of the then President of Brazil.

One day a few weeks later I strolled over to the Children's
Hospital from the School of Religion where I was teaching.
Arthur Steindler was pacing up and down a corridor, his
eyes half closed, his face drawn as though in great pain. I
asked one of the staff what was wrong. "Nothing," was the
reply. "After a heavy operating schedule, the doctor always
looks that way. He suffers pain along with his patients—especially the children."

They call it empathy. I have never seen anyone share the
anguish of his patients as intensely as Dr. Steindler. He once
lectured before a learned medical society on "The Symphony
of Pain." The Iowa surgeon wanted his colleagues to remember always that they were treating not just muscles, bones,
tendons, and ligaments, but human beings who suffered.

It was easy to understand why his "boys" worshiped him.
He knew more about the human body—its anatomical structure, its physiological workings, its pathology—than almost
any other man. He was a walking medical encyclopedia.
And he was full of compassion. Often, the score of surgeons
who trailed him down a hallway waited while their master
paused to speak to a scrubwoman cleaning the walls. "Hello,
Mrs. Jones; has your husband gotten over his cold yet?"

In the wards, youngsters in traction and in casts put out
their fingers or toes for the doctor to touch as he walked

by their beds. They knew his was no contrived bedside manner, that his heart as well as his mind and supple hands belonged to them.

Item 2. An interview with a former Steindler student, now a surgeon in Cincinnati, who reminisced about his former teacher. Next to his passion for healing, and possibly on a par with it, was his eagerness to communicate his insights to others. Whether through the printed word, the classroom lecture, or in clinic discussion, Dr. Steindler had an overwhelming urge to share his medical discoveries. There was more than a touch of genius in his teaching. He showed his students how to get one muscle to do the work of another, useless one. The textbooks call it "the Steindler physiological tendon transplant." If, as a result of disease or injury, the patient could not bend his thumb, Steindler would shift another muscle around it, so that, for example, the extensor would assume the job of the flexor. Usually, the thumb could be made to work as good as new.

Most famous men develop a kind of remoteness, a barrier created by awe, which keeps their students at a respectful distance. Steindler enjoyed surrounding himself in an intimate way with his young associates and students. At prewedding parties, he served as toastmaster and discoursed humorously on "The Difficult Art of Marriage." He often took lunch with the "boys" to probe into their problems. And even late into the evening, they felt free to call at his home to present a particularly perplexing medical matter.

Dr. Steindler was in a real sense the father of orthopedic surgeons—virtually an "alma mater" in himself. Almost a sixth of the 2,000 qualified American bone surgeons received all or part of their training under him. The Arthur Steindler Alumni Association, an elite group of over 300 orthopedic surgeons practicing in most of the United States and in a dozen foreign countries, still meets every year to discuss their work and to recount stories about their master.

Item 3. A profile in an old copy of the *Des Moines Register*. Arthur Steindler was born in Austria, son of a distinguished jurist. His mother, too, was an able attorney. All four Steindler children had doctor's degrees. His two sisters were among the first of their sex to receive doctorates at the University of Vienna.

The young medical student came under the spell of the great Dr. Adolf Lorenz, one of the pioneers of orthopedic surgery. Inspired by his example, Arthur determined to devote his life to the maimed and the crippled. His native Austria was not too hospitable to Jewish surgeons, however, and in 1907 the young doctor decided to emigrate to America.

The turning point in Arthur Steindler's life came soon after he began practicing in Des Moines, Iowa. The State legislature passed the Perkins Law in 1913, and Dr. Steindler was invited to open an orthopedic clinic under its regulations. Few people outside Iowa are familiar with the magnificent medical facilities made possible for every resident of the state under the provisions of the Perkins Law. A visitor to the University of Iowa Hospital, coming at dawn, can see a large fleet of sleek ambulances streaming from the medical center to every corner of the state. They are scheduled to pick up a youngster in Mason City, near the Minnesota border, or a farmer 350 miles away at the South Dakota line. The resident of an old folks' home not far from Missouri will be brought back that evening to receive the best care which modern medical science can offer. I have seen an inmate of the Iowa State Penitentiary, on temporary leave, enter to undergo surgery.

The shiny super-ambulances of today are a far cry from the first vehicle used for transporting patients. The early ambulances looked like the wagons used by itinerant scissors grinders. But they brought the sick and the crippled to Iowa City where, without charge or at minimum cost, they enjoyed the benefits ordinarily found only at the Mayo Clinic or Johns Hopkins Medical Center. It wasn't long until every farmer in Iowa knew the name of Steindler.

The newspaper account told of a thirty-one-year-old polio victim who hadn't taken a step since he was ten. After a series of treatments and operations, he walked out of the Children's Hospital with perfect ease.

Beulah, a pretty sixteen-year-old girl from a small central Iowa town, had been hurt in a basketball game when she crashed into a wall. She went into a six-week coma. The diagnosis: encephalitis—sleeping sickness. One medical specialist suggested that she be kept permanently in a wheel chair, since she would always look grotesque, even if she were able to learn a little locomotion. When Dr. Steindler took over the case, he infused new hope into the family. It required forty operations, but Beulah was finally able to walk, using only a cane. Today, happily married, she is the proud mother of three fine, healthy children.

Lucille, an Indian girl of seventeen, was a high diver in a carnival passing through Iowa. Somehow her diving board was placed at the shallow end of the tank, and in the accident, she became completely paralyzed. After some time she regained use of her arms. But her legs remained immobile until Dr. Steindler took charge.

Treatment was long and tedious, and the county authorities who were paying for Lucille's care grew impatient at the prolonged burden. But the doctor pleaded her cause, begging them to see him through until she could become a useful, self-supporting person.

To the doors of the Children's Hospital were brought some of nature's weirdest mistakes. A woman whose thighs and knees were monstrous in size, as though drawn on the crayon book of a four-year-old. Or a young boy whose feet faced backward instead of forward. And an endless parade of polio victims, muscular dystrophy and osteomyelitis patients, arthritics, and men and women with limp hands, useless feet.

Almost every summer, Dr. Steindler traveled to the Continent, and returned with new ideas and new methods to correct deformities. He was one of the first to operate on infants four to six months old for club feet. At this time the bone is mostly cartilage, and it is possible to correct the disability before the child is ready to walk.

ITEM 4. An interview with Thea, Dr. Steindler's secretary of twenty years standing, now living in Silver Springs, Maryland. In the early days Arthur Steindler would bring home with him to spend several weeks as a family guest a patient who faced extended treatment. Arthur had married Louise, a nurse whom he met in Chicago. The Steindler home was blessed with devotion, but not with children of their own. It was never an empty house, however, for in the wake of Nazi persecution, a steady stream of refugees were brought to Iowa City—nieces, nephews, cousins. The Steindlers added a wing to their gracious home to accommodate them.

It was more than a home, it was a hostel. One girl meeting another in the hallway asked, "Who are you?"

"I'm one of the folks living here," was the answer.

"So am I."

The pace Dr. Steindler set for himself was breathless. He arose between 4:30 and 5 A.M., took a two-mile walk, even in rain, snow, or sleet, and breakfasted at six. Until he gave up his university duties, he would dictate into his dictaphone for an hour, preparing lectures and his next book. At seven he began rounds of surgery, teaching, hospital visitations, clinic supervision.

Every morning Dr. Steindler would drive up to the Children's Hospital in his old Essex, medical students draped on the running boards and crammed into every bit of space inside the doctor's car. On his face a wide happy grin showed his pride in his precious, gay cargo.

His keen desire to help others was a lifetime passion. At the outbreak of World War I, as an immigrant doctor, he pleaded with the Army to use his services, but technically he was ineligible, for he had been born in Austria—enemy territory. Waiting for the Army to change its mind, Arthur Steindler traveled to various cities, performing operations in place of surgeons who had gone to war, and turning his fees over to their wives and families.

The Army finally relented, and he rose in short order to the rank of Lieutenant Colonel in the Reserves. As a pioneer in military medicine, Steindler was asked some interesting questions by the Army: "What is the gait or pace that will best conserve a dogfoot's energies?" "What is the maximum weight a GI can carry on his back without injury?" (The average infantryman, especially Bill Mauldin, is sure that he came up with a much too optimistic answer.)

The Army sent him to Massachusetts shoe factories to help design the type of shoe most helpful to the weary soldier. (He wrote a monograph showing that the "shoulders back, chest out, stomach in" posture the Army demanded was biologically unwise, perhaps harmful. The Army apparently decided to stay with the virile, though unhealthy, position nevertheless.)

Steindler was always eager to share his medical discoveries with people all over the world, and his at-homeness in many languages helped. It was not unusual for the doctor to deliver a series of lectures in fluent Spanish in Mexico City, address the Belgian Orthopedic Association in French a short time later, and lecture on other occasions in Czech, German, Hungarian, or Italian with equal ease.

ITEM 5. My last visit with Dr. Steindler. He was then seventy-six years old, had chalked up over 30,000 surgical operations, and was nearing the end of a wonderfully full lifetime. The doctor stopped in New York on his way to London, to be honored by the British Royal College of Surgeons. I asked him when he could be reached the following day at his hotel room.

"Oh, call me at five . . ."

"Will you be back at the hotel by five P.M.?"

"I mean five A.M.!" he replied, without batting an eye.

Arthur Steindler is still a subject of research for me. In my travels, I continue to meet his disciples, many of them eminent surgeons who have tried, in some measure, to fashion their lives after his.

Sometimes, too, when I am tempted to separate myself from the pain of others and to persuade myself that a clergyman or a doctor cannot bear too personally the burdens of misery and grief of the countless numbers who seek their help, I see the Iowa doctor's countenance before me, mirroring the hurt on the face of a crippled child, and I say to my hesitant self: "You can do no less."

# Partners in Creation

I AM HAUNTED by a statistic I read the other day: *Infant Mortality Rate*—100 per cent. The source is a UNESCO study, and the reference is to a remote village in the interior of Brazil.

If I understand the figures and the notes accompanying them correctly, they indicate that disease and poor nutrition doom every single child in that benighted village to death before adulthood. Nor is this an isolated, unique situation. In all of Latin America the same study reveals only 40 per cent of the children receive any kind of schooling. The majority are condemned from birth to illiteracy and intellectual paralysis, perpetual by-products of the grinding poverty that will continue to enslave them all their lives. And as things now stand, the situation will get worse in these underdeveloped, over-populated lands as the birth rate continues to spiral out of bounds.

We who are heirs to the Judaeo-Christian tradition are now asking ourselves if we cannot find some way to prevent the "population explosion" from destroying our hopes for the future even while we labor to avoid a more lethal explosion. For the answer to this pressing issue, if answer there is, must come from our midst.

Dr. Richard Fagley, leading Protestant authority on population trends, recently called upon the World Council of Churches to consider the Protestant responsibility in this challenge. Does Judaism have anything to say?

When I visited the Middle East, I was overwhelmed, as are all travelers, by the sheer numbers that surged all around me, wherever I turned. How can human values be preserved, I asked myself, when so many people are pressing against one another for the barest essentials of living?

Our ancient Jewish concept of each human being individually hand-tooled by our Creator seems to falter in a world so abundantly peopled. The suggestion of mass production is almost inescapable in the statistics that assail us. Doesn't the very quality of humanness suffer when there are too many of us? Surely man, as God's creation, can exercise the choice with which God endowed him to determine with thoughtful care how many children he shall bring into this world.

"Planned parenthood" is still a matter of controversy in many quarters, but everything in the spirit of Judaism cries out for sanctioning that principle. Judaism prizes the quality of life above all else. Man is better than the beast of the field because of his capacity for nobility, for compassion, for imagination. A society which shackles itself to conditions of life that degrade the human spirit denies these differences and is therefore evil. There can be no immorality in man's efforts to free himself from such cruel enslavement.

Judaism has no "ideal" number of children: Some families find fulfillment in six or eight; others feel that they can do greatest justice to one or two. Jewish tradition does suggest that each family has a moral obligation to perpetuate itself— that is, through two children. But size, spacing, and other considerations are wholly subjective. Suffusing Jewish life through the centuries is a passion for wholesome parent-child relationships and an expectation of happiness in the bond between husband and wife. A home in which the pressures of children's needs are economic burdens so overwhelm the parents that they have little time or opportunity to relate to each other in a rewarding way cannot possibly achieve this ideal.

During my university teaching days, many faculty couples practiced "academic spacing." By planning their children at four-year intervals, they hoped to spare themselves the burden of having to put two children through college at one time.

Even this campus foresight failed if the older child decided to go on to graduate work or professional school. Only the most wise among us, says the Talmud, can see things yet unborn. Nevertheless, planning is a concept congenial to the Jewish spirit. For planning implies an application of our God-given wisdom and intellect to our human problems. Because we humans are the only earthly creatures endowed with the understanding and imagination to plan and project for the future, we dare to consider ourselves partners in the divine enterprise, including the act of procreation.

The moral problem inherent in the "population explosion" is two-dimensional—it involves both the present and the future. In our own lifetime, those of us "privileged" with the scientific knowhow to control unwanted parenthood, have a solemn obligation to share such knowledge with the hundreds of millions who still dwell in darkness.

True, there are some who maintain that there is no clear and present danger to humanity as long as our capacity for food production does not lag behind our productivity. But our ethical obligation is not limited in this way. Man who shares, in some measure, God's gift of timelessness, has a solemn obligation to plan and provide for generations beyond the horizon of his own experience.

The "population explosion" is a product of man's intellectual and moral genius, not merely his biological prowess. For the vast increase in our numbers results not only from geometric progression but also from a decreasing infant mortality, the conquest of many diseases, and a greater acceptance and tolerance of the physically afflicted.

Thus we can see in the proliferation of life a tribute to our gifts of mind and heart. But, by the same token, if life in abundance does not bring in its wake the abundant life, mankind must harness all of its creative resources to organize a society in which each family can control its own destiny and seek its own self-fulfillment.

# Rabbis in a Child's Mirror

THE RABBI'S SELF-IMAGE is easily punctured, especially by the candid tongue of the young. A rabbi lacking in humility can acquire it with dispatch listening to a youngster's comments about him.

Robed in glistening white, the rabbi ascends the altar for a Yom Kippur service, feeling resplendent and high-priestlike. A four-year-old whispers to his older sister: "Why does the rabbi wear a lady's housecoat in the temple?"

The Torah rites begin—and the rabbi intones the words of the Psalmist:

"Who shall ascend the mountain of the Lord, and who shall stand in His Holy place? He that hath clean hands . . ."

A squeaky voice reaches the rabbi's ears:

"Clean hands? Phooey!"

Rabbinic authority does not assert itself until the Sunday school student reaches the age of reason—usually around the tenth grade.

I invited my confirmation class to review my book as though it were to appear in the *New York Times Book Review* section. One review began with these words: "*What Is a Jew* was written by our rabbi, and the facts contained in the book are straight from the horse's mouth."

The Hindu poet Tagore likened youth to a green apple, juicy and tart. But sometimes there is a sweet compassion which the adult world cannot match. The youngster in the age of discovery perceives relationships unseen by sophisticated eyes, and is capable of a sensitivity beyond the reach of calloused years.

One evening, I was driving seven-year-old Martha to her home, when she noticed me yawning. It had been a long arduous day, typical of the exhausting schedule of the ministry.

"You tired, Rabbi?"

"Yes, Martha, I am."

"You know what I think? I think our temple should have a day rabbi and a night rabbi, like in a hospital."

# The Talmud's Lighter Side—or—
# Is That in the Talmud?

A FRIEND OF MINE, a busy college president, once asked me where he could learn more about the Talmud. He had heard rabbis quote from it, and had been struck by its humaneness, its relevant modernity, and its picturesque speech. Could a layman read a translation of the Talmud?

I explained that much of the Talmud is dull reading—as is the Book of Statutes or any other legal tome. For essentially the core of the Talmud is law and legal discussion. But interlaced are thousands of anecdotes, biographical profiles and charming parables that make the Jews of the first five centuries come alive as human beings—good and bad, brilliant and insipid, solemn and frivolous. It is this kind of material that is available in popular anthologies.

A seemingly ponderous discussion of the law provides a timeless nugget of perception. In one instance, for example, in determining guilt for a criminal offense, the rabbis say, "The mouse is not the thief—the hole is the thief." Many centuries passed before the rest of us began to assess the role of environment, of society itself, in creating conditions conducive to crime.

The pastoral setting of that ancient world reflects clearly in the colorful vocabulary of the ancient scholars who combined work in the fields with their study in the academies. The thought that there is greater satisfaction in giving than receiving has been frequently stated, but never more vividly than in the suggestion: "More than you want the milk, the cow wants to give it."

I find a particular joy of recognition when I discover an ancient root for a familiar expression. Not long ago, I came across a note in the Talmud which declared: "He falls asleep and dreams of far-off Spain." My curiosity piqued, I tried to find the origin of the phrase "castles in Spain." It appears in the work of a seventeenth-century English writer and there is an earlier allusion in fourteenth-century Chaucer. But why Spain? Why not Italy, or remote India? The answer, I think, lies in the distance from the original writer's abode. Spain may be fairly close to London, it's true. But to the Talmudic scholar in Babylonia, it represented the very edge of the world.

One of the most interesting aspects of the Bible lies in the fact that there is no attempt to gloss over the seamy side of illustrious Jewish leaders. Take, for example, the astonishing account of King David's blemishes, especially his dereliction in the matter of Bath-sheba. Surely, the royal authorities who permitted the record to stand must have felt uncomfortable about preserving for posterity the foibles of their ancestors. Even our own democratic press tends to protect its leaders with a degree of self-imposed censorship. Not so the Talmud, which, like the Bible, evidently regarded every facet of rabbinic news as "fit to print."

In contrast with the vapid puritanism of medieval times, the Talmud dealt with marriage in human, often idyllic terms. Romance and compatibility were considered essential ingredients of a good marriage. "No place is too crowded for a couple in love," the wise men wrote, two thousand years ago. The wife of Rabbi Meir, one of the giants of the Talmudic Age, was described as a woman who shared his intellectual interests and to whom he was tied in a bond of mutual adoration.

"He who has a good wife," the Talmud asserts, "has God for a father-in-law." At another point we find the warning: "Don't make your wife weep, for God counts her tears."

Furthermore, wrote the sages: "No matter how tall you are, or how short your wife is, lean down and listen to her advice."

But since every one of the thousands of pages was written by a male scholar, gallantry was always tempered by a sense of masculine superiority, hidden at times behind a glint of humor. There are the legends, for example, about the world's beginning, which depict the angels flying overhead, dropping souls and whispering into the ears of newborn babies the names of their destined husbands or wives (which explains love at first sight). One such legend reports that the angel in charge of conversation was dispatched to earth with ten bagfuls of talking. His distribution was faulty, the legend declares. Only one bag of talking was opened by men and the nine remaining went to the women.

Then there is the staid rabbi-scholar who bewails his marital lot: What a shrew he has for a wife! When he feels like having lentil soup for lunch, he asks for something else, and out of spite she gives him lentil soup!

The double standard which still characterizes today's Oriental society was clearly evident among the Jews of ancient Israel and Babylonia. Certainly the laws of divorce were drawn up to benefit the husband. Despite numerous legal disabilities, however, there is no question that women were greatly revered. The character of the home, the ancients declared, was determined by the quality of the wife and mother. The Talmud tells of a pious God-fearing couple who could not have children. They were divorced. The pious man married a mean woman, and he forthwith became wicked. The pious woman married a mean man and he forthwith became pious.

Even such seemingly trivial subjects as a woman's make-up are touched upon in the Talmud. Though the Bible preached that "Grace is deceitful, and beauty is vain," and Isaiah denounced the lavish cosmetics of the ladies of Jerusalem, Judaism has never interpreted these injunctions to mean that women may not make the most of their endowments. "She wears no make-up, neither on her eyes, her cheeks, nor on her lips, but she is a rare beauty," declares the Talmud in describing a particular woman. Let it not be said that the ancient Israelites didn't recognize beauty when they saw it!

The most astounding law in the entire Talmud, I think, is found in a passage dealing with the Sabbath. Traditional law forbids a Jew to engage in any labor on the Sabbath that involves adding to or subtracting from the growth process. Plowing a field or cutting the grass, even the paring of fingernails is prohibited. One may not add a nail to a house, for that is building.

But, ask the rabbis, what about a woman putting on make-up? Does that violate the Sabbath? The answer is simple and clear. Since it is important for a woman to look good on the Sabbath, she may use cosmetics to improve her face!

But, asks one rabbi, with obvious tongue in cheek, this may hold true for a young woman, but how about a woman who gets to be old? The gallant answer is thunderously offered: No woman is too old to be uninterested in how she looks.

The entire discussion in the ancient Babylonian Academy seems to run counter to the traditional Jewish emphasis on the nonphysical. Hebraism, unlike Hellenism, eschewed the objective arts, and saw in them an element of paganism. But as the stern Hebraism of a desert people gave way to greater sophistication, its thinkers differentiated between a preoccupation with physical form for its own sake—which they branded as idolatry—and a healthy regard for natural and man-made beauty, especially if it reflected an inner beauty of soul.

The Hebrew word *chen* carries this double connotation. A person possessed of *chen*, like the Greek charisma, has charm, an inborn grace, and with it all a distinct physical attractiveness.

The Talmud, in considering the qualifications for a judge, declares that a person who sits on the bench must be sufficiently prepossessing in appearance to elicit respect. A Hollywood matinee idol? No. In Yiddish, the phrase, *a shayner yid* (a fine-looking Jew) does not refer to an Adonis with a classic profile but to a person whose face, bearing, and inner nobility automatically evoke respect. On the scale of Jewish values, Lincoln was an inordinately "handsome" man.

Historic Judaism had none of the trappings of modern sociology and psychology, but it knew a great deal about the subtleties of the mind. "The heart does not always confide in the lips," declared one of the rabbis.

These little glimpses into the Talmud are in no sense an introduction into the mainstream of its thought; they merely touch its fringes. I hope, though, that they offer some understanding of the remarkable sensitivity of the ancient Jewish world in the matter of human relationships and the workings of the heart.

# A Final Thought

CRITICS OF MARTIN BUBER have often argued that his interpretations of Hasidic teachings are not entirely authentic, and that the noted philosopher uses a sieve instead of transmitting the lessons of the Hasidim in their pristine form. Dr. Buber has a somewhat different explanation. "I don't *use* a sieve," he declares; "I *am* a sieve."

All of us, I think, share this desire to take from our tradition that which we regard as its essence, to pluck out the relevant, the pertinent, those elements of revelation which move us. We are all, in Buber's terms, sieves for that which is meaningful in our past.

Does this make our faith a wholly subjective thing? Not at all. Visitors to the British National Gallery, for instance, cannot possibly carry away equally clear impressions of all its paintings. One person remembers most vividly a particular Rembrandt; another is most moved by a Gainsborough or a Reynolds. Both impressions are equally precious and for both viewers there is the sense of much more in the background, yet to be enjoyed. So it is with our faith.

In the writings and teachings of Judaism, three thousand years of human experience have been detailed for us with warmth and sensitivity. There is vision enough in that record for all who have the desire to see.

## ABOUT THE AUTHOR

Morris N. Kertzer has been teacher, preacher, pastor, and author on the "art" of his faith both for Jews and for the non-Jewish community engaged in interfaith relations.

Author of *With an H on My Dog Tag,* based on his service as the sole Jewish chaplain at Anzio, Dr. Kertzer also wrote the best-selling *What Is a Jew?*

A former college professor, associated in his early rabbinic career with the distinguished Dr. Milton Steinberg and Director of Interreligious Affairs for the American Jewish Committee, Rabbi Kertzer was called back to the pulpit in 1960, when he became spiritual leader of the Larchmont Temple.

His influence on the community outside his congregation has continued and Dr. Kertzer in 1962 was invited to speak in South America on "The Jewish Message in the Face of the Present Problems of Man." He was a guest also of the Jewish-Christian Fraternity of Brazil when he addressed the clergy, religious educators, and journalists on "Insights and Experiences for Interfaith."

Rabbi Kertzer received the Pro Deo Gold Medal in Rome for his work in promoting Catholic-Jewish understanding and the George Washington Medal of 1956 for his analysis of Soviet anti-Semitism. He is Chairman of the Church-State Commission and a member of the Executive Council of the Central Conference of American Rabbis, and is featured columnist and editorial aid for the *Jewish Digest.*

*This book was set in*

*Caledonia and Janson types by*

*Harry Sweetman Typesetting Corporation.*

*It was printed and bound at the press of*

*The World Publishing Company.*

*Design is by Larry Kamp.*